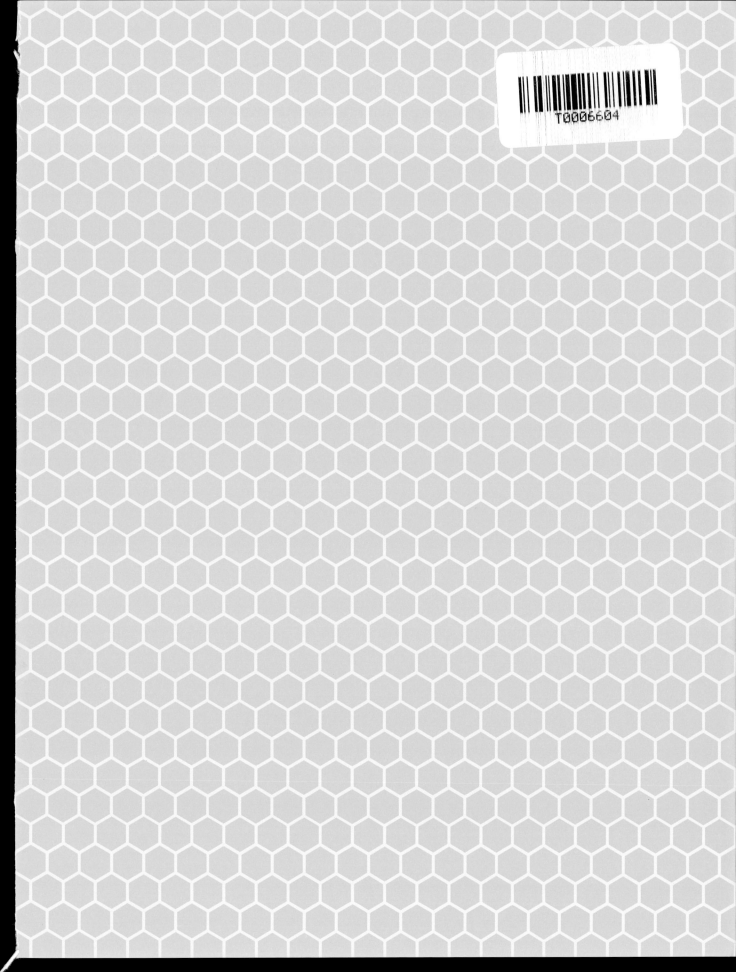

The Book of Bees

Inside the Hives and Lives of HONEYBEES, BUMBLEBEES, CUCKOO BEES, and Other BUSY BUZZERS

Lela Nargi

BLACK DOG
& LEVENTHAL
PUBLISHERS
NEW YORK

Text copyright © 2022 by Black Dog & Leventhal Publishers

Print book interior design by Kevin Knight

Cover design by Kevin Knight

Black Dog & Leventhal Publishers
Hachette Book Group
1290 Avenue of the Americas
New York, NY 10104

www.hachettebookgroup.com
www.blackdogandleventhal.com

First Edition: March 2022

Produced by Girl Friday Productions, Seattle
www.girlfridayproductions.com

Black Dog & Leventhal Publishers is an imprint of Perseus Books, LLC, a subsidiary of Hachette Book Group, Inc. The Black Dog & Leventhal Publishers name and logo are trademarks of Hachette Book Group, Inc.

The Hachette Speakers Bureau provides a wide range of authors for speaking events. To find out more, go to www.HachetteSpeakersBureau.com or call (866) 376-6591.

Library of Congress Cataloging-in-Publication Data has been applied for.
ISBNs: 978-0-7624-7840-8 (hardcover);
978-0-7624-7841-5 (ebook)

Printed in China
APS

10 9 8 7 6 5 4 3 2 1

Contents

Introduction

We live on a planet ruled by insects. There are more of these six-legged creatures than anything else on Earth. In fact, there are 900,000 species, or different kinds, of them. About 20,000 of these species are bees.

Some bees are so tiny you almost need a microscope to see them. Some are big enough to fit in the palm of your hand. They all share a wasp ancestor that existed millions of years ago.

Bees drink flower nectar and many types also collect *pollen*, the dustlike grains inside flowers. To allow them to transport pollen back to their hives for food, these bees have hairs all over their bodies to help pollen stick to them. The pollen-collecting hairs on their legs are called *scopa*.

Not all bees collect pollen; the ones that don't are hairless. Some bees even feed meat to their babies instead of pollen or nectar. But all bees start as eggs that turn into larvae, then pupae, then adults.

Some bees live in holes in wood. Some live in wax hives. Others live in holes in the ground. Most bees like their *habitats*, or the places where they live, to be warm and dry. But some bees don't mind it chilly and damp. Many bees are *solitary*—they live alone. Some bees are *social*, and they live in groups called *colonies*. Colonies have queen bees that only lay eggs while the other females do everything else. Bees that live in colonies make honey, but solitary bees don't. They dry flower nectar in their hives until it is thick. Only honeybees make enough honey to share with humans.

Some bees live in between solitary and colony life. They are sort of solitary, but females make their nests close to each other. Sometimes they even help each other build.

Bees may collect nectar and pollen from different types of flowers. These are *generalist* bees. Other bees collect nectar and pollen from just one type of flower. These are *specialist* bees. When we talk about *native* bees, we mean bees that come from the place where you find them, just like you may be a native New Yorker or Los Angeleno or Mexican. Other bees are *introduced*. They were brought from one place to another. Some may even be *invasive*. That means they took over the new place from the native bees that lived there, and now no one can get rid of them.

Scientists think this is one reason native bees in some places are disappearing. They are rare so they are becoming *endangered* and scientists worry that they may go extinct—and some are *extinct* already. Or they may be *threatened*, meaning they might soon become endangered. How can you help? Get to know some of these amazing insects on the pages of this book. Look for them when you go outside. Then work to make the world around you better for bees. We'll even tell you how!

▶ *A western honeybee collects nectar and pollen from a coneflower.*

The Wide World of Bees and How We Identify Them

In a lot of ways, the 20,000 species of bees worldwide are alike. All bees have four wings. They all have a head, a thorax, and an abdomen that are clearly separate (see Bees at a Glance, page 54). They have two *compound eyes* on the sides of their heads. They have three simple eyes on the tops of their heads. They have antennae, mouthparts with a tongue, and jaws called *mandibles*. They might have a few teeth or a lot of them.

HOW TO ID BEES

How can you tell one bee from another? This can be tricky. Even scientists sometimes have a hard time telling them apart. In the bee profiles throughout this book, you'll get to look at the similarities and differences among species of bees. But sometimes, we need to do more research on hard-to-identify bees. One way is to practice—researchers spend lots of time studying bee species around the world. Another way is to get to know their *taxonomy*. A taxonomy is a system for arranging living things into smaller and smaller groups. It's kind of like a family tree.

This beekeeper is dressed for success (in collecting honey from the hives, that is).

THE FAMILY TREE OF TAXONOMY

Here's how bees fit in on that tree:

Kingdom   Animalia (all animals, including rhinos and penguins)
Phylum   Arthropoda (animals with exoskeletons, such as spiders and lobsters)
Class   Insecta (bugs!)
Order   Hymenoptera (ants, bees, sawflies and wasps)
Family   Hymenoptera with common ancestor
Genus   Closely related bees (such as all honeybees)
Species   Bees that are similar enough to mate with each other
Subspecies   Species with regional differences

INSIDE THE HIVE: What Happens in a Honeybee Colony

Bees certainly keep busy, but a lot of their activity happens inside the hive or nest. Mason bees are solitary, but peek inside the hive of communal bees, and you'll find hundreds, maybe even thousands, of bees all working together to support their colony. To do that, each bee has a job:

Queen: In each colony of bees, there is one queen whose job it is to lay all the eggs for the hive. Some queen bees will lay up to 2 million eggs in their lifetime!

Drone bees: In a hive with tens of thousands of bees, only about 100 are males, also known as *drones*. You can pick them out in a crowded hive by their bigger bodies and huge eyes. These guys have just one job: mate with the queen. That's all they do—they're otherwise fed and cared for by *worker* bees.

Worker bees: Every single bee in a colony that's not a queen bee or a drone is a worker bee. All worker bees are female, and they do everything but lay eggs or mate. Worker bees will have several jobs in their lives:

- Cleaner: Someone needs to keep the hive tidy!
- Nurse: These worker bees take care of eggs and larva.
- Fanner: They help transform nectar into honey by fanning it with their wings.
- Nectar mover: These bees take nectar from foragers and deposit it in cells.
- Wax maker: When they're about two weeks old, worker bees' bodies start producing wax flakes. They use this to build new cells and seal off the ones filled with honey.
- Guard: These workers defend the hive from invaders.
- Forager: These worker bees fly out in search of pollen and nectar, then bring it back to the hive.

LET'S DANCE!

When a forager bee finds a great source of nectar, she'll fly back to the hive to tell her fellow foragers. How does she do this? She busts a move! Honeybee foragers do a special bee dance, or waggle. Each dance move communicates directions (left, right, straight ahead) and distance (three feet, two miles, or even more) to the nectar.

▶ *Honeybees inside their hive. Can you spot the queen?*

◀ *Dwarf honeybees (Apis florea) resting on the outside of their hive.*

HONEYBEES

Family: Apidae
Genus: *Apis*

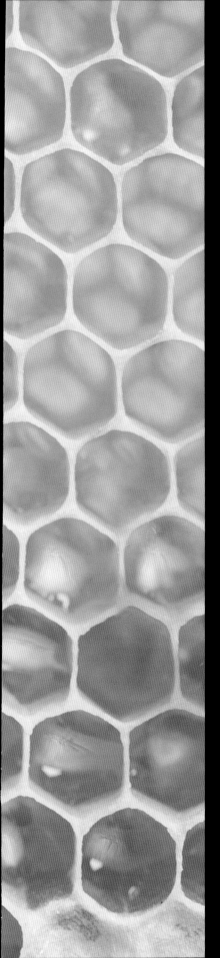

When people think of bees, they usually think of honeybees. In fact, the Latin word for a honeybee—*apis*—means "bee." Humans and honeybees have a long history together. For thousands of years, we have *domesticated* them, raising them for honey. Archaeologists have even found honey in ancient Egyptian tombs. For about 100 years, commercial beekeepers have raised honeybees too. They rent them to farmers to pollinate crops.

Ancient cultures, such as the Mayans, kept other types of bees for honey, especially some of the 500 species of stingless bees. But most of us today get our honey from two species of honeybees called *Apis mellifera* and *Apis cerana*.

There are six other species of honeybees. Two are medium size, just like *Apis mellifera* and *Apis cerana*. Two are huge (*Megapis*), and two are tiny (*Micrapis*). In total, there are 44 subspecies of honeybees. Not one of them is native to North America.

Honeybee species are a lot alike. They all have queens, worker females, and male drones. Female workers have barbed stingers. Queens have *ovipositors*—used for laying eggs—instead. Male drones have no stingers and no ovipositors. Instead, each one has an *endophallus* for mating with the queen.

All honeybee species are *social* and live together in colonies in wax hives. They also have hairy bodies and even hairy eyeballs to help them collect pollen. They are *superorganisms*. That means the colony itself is like one big organism made up of bees. One bee cannot survive without all the other bees.

◀ *Busy worker bees.*

Western honeybee
(also known as the *European honeybee*)

Apis mellifera

ID THIS BEE

This is a slim, medium-size honeybee. It is golden yellow with dark-brown, blackish stripes. These bees dangle their legs as they fly.

BOXES OF BEES

Bees kept by beekeepers build honeycombs on special boards. Beekeepers store the boards in boxes so that they are easy to pull out for collecting honey. Boxes also make it easy for beekeepers to move bees around. Some people keep bees in the backyard. *Commercial beekeepers* truck bees all over the country to work for farmers. Honeybees are generalists and are happy to visit almond and apple orchards. And blueberry and broccoli farms. And squash patches and cranberry bogs.

BEE-HAVIOR

If you are from North America, you often see *Apis mellifera* in gardens and parks. They are the only honeybees around. But these bees are immigrants. They were brought over by Europeans back in the 1600s. Why? Because they are great pollinators. A colony of honeybees can pollinate a lot of food crops. They also make a *loooot* of honey. It is their main food. But they can make enough for beekeepers to share.

One honeybee queen makes all the babies in the colony. She lives for two or three years. A few thousand male drones live for three months. They have one job, although only 5 or 10 of them are lucky enough to do it. They mate with the queen. Up to 60,000 female workers do *everything else* for the colony. They protect it. (That is why workers have stingers—ouch!) They raise the babies. They clean. They feed the queen. They collect pollen and nectar. A worker can fly eight miles in a day and visit 1,000 flowers.

All these bees live together in a hive built of wax. This comes from wax glands in a worker bee's abdomen. A bee chews the wax to soften it, and then she spits it out and forms it into a honeycomb. Workers in the wild build honeycombs inside tree hollows or caves.

WHERE?
Europe, Middle East, Africa

SIZE
Female worker: 0.4–0.6 inch (10–15 mm) long

Queen: 0.8 inch (20 mm) long

Male: 0.7 inch

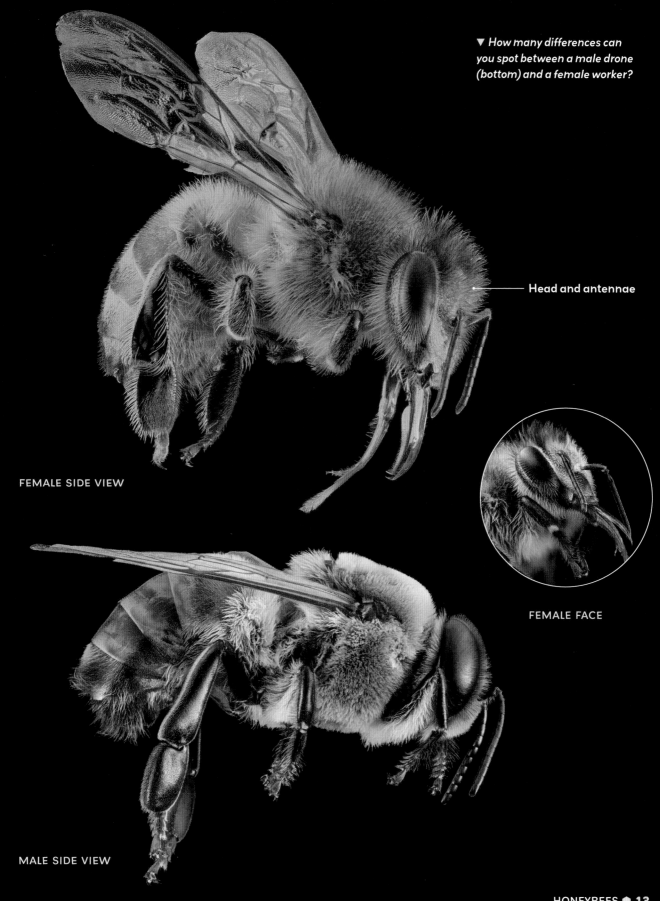

▼ *How many differences can you spot between a male drone (bottom) and a female worker?*

Head and antennae

FEMALE SIDE VIEW

FEMALE FACE

MALE SIDE VIEW

Asiatic honeybee
Apis cerana

ID THIS BEE

This honeybee looks and acts a lot like *Apis mellifera*. It is black, with four yellow abdominal stripes. Queens are bigger and darker colored.

HOW TO HANDLE A HORNET

Sometimes a hornet invades an *Apis cerana* hive. Then the females work together to do something special. They surround the hornet in a tight ball. They start to vibrate. This raises the heat inside to 122 degrees Fahrenheit (50 degrees Celsius). That's hot enough to kill the hornet but not hot enough to harm the bees. It is called *heat balling*. It is kind of like a superpower.

BEE-HAVIOR

For 9,000 years, humans have eaten honey from honeybees. We've collected their wax to make things like candles and lip balm. We raise them to pollinate our crops. Our lives would be less sweet—and we would be a lot hungrier—without honeybees.

Asiatic honeybees are the same shape and color as western honeybees (*Apis mellifera*). They have other things in common too. For example, workers collect pollen on their bodies and legs and eyes. They collect nectar by slurping it with their tongues. They roll pollen and nectar together into balls, then carry the balls home in "baskets" on the backs of their legs. The scientific word for this basket is *corbicula*.

Asiatic honeybees live all over Asia. They can survive in hot places and cold places, in dry places and wet places, and at high and low altitudes. The higher up in the mountains the bees live, the bigger they are.

Honeybees build nests out of wax inside tree cavities. Each nest contains a special room shaped like a peanut. Only queens are raised inside it.

Like all honeybees, Asiatic honeybees forage in many types of flowers. They are generalists. They are important pollinators of coconuts, spices, mangos, cashews, and guava. Yum!

WHERE?

Southern Asia into Russia, Australia

SIZE

Female worker: 0.3–0.35 inch (7–9 mm) long

Queen: 0.4 inch (11 mm) long

Male drone: 0.35–0.4 inch (9–10 mm) long

Four yellow
abdominal stripes

FEMALE SIDE VIEW

FEMALE FACE

MALE SIDE VIEW

▲ *A female* Apis cerana *has a longer abdomen than a male.*

Asian giant honeybee
Apis dorsata

ID THIS BEE

Their color varies from place to place. But some of these honeybees have a golden-yellow thorax and black abdomen with white stripes. This is one of the biggest bees around. It is twice as long as *Apis mellifera*.

ON THE MOVE

Fall means the monsoon season, or the rainy season, in many tropical places. That's when *Apis dorsata* bees migrate, moving with the seasons. They may travel for two months and up to 125 miles (200 km) to make the most of newly blooming flowers. They stop to rest on tree branches. They also stop to eat pollen and nectar along the way. When the time is right, they migrate back the way they came. Scientists think they may even return to their old nests. But sadly, because forests are being cut down—called *deforestation*—these bees have less of the land and food they need to survive.

BEE-HAVIOR

Apis dorsata isn't just bigger than other honeybees. It does cool stuff others don't.

For starters, these bees don't bother to hide their nests inside hollow trees. Instead, they build honeycombs on tree branches and underneath cliffs, right out in the open. The combs hang like big droopy drips. Sometimes there are 50 big droopy drips hanging from the same "bee tree." Sometimes the combs are 75 feet (23 m) in the air.

The *brood* of baby bees is snug inside the comb. Honey and pollen are also stored inside. Thousands of worker bees cover the whole outside of the comb. This protects the contents of the comb, even from wind and rain. Also safe: as much as 33 pounds (15 kg) of honey.

Beekeepers tried for a long time to domesticate this species. It did not work. So instead, locals climb a bee tree in the middle of the night to harvest wild *Apis dorsata* honey. It is dangerous for the humans because of the height and because they are sometimes attacked by tigers. And it is dangerous for the bees because sometimes the humans knock down whole hives.

Apis dorsata bees live in tropical places. They forage in many kinds of tropical plants. They are very important pollinators of mangos and litchis, lemons and star fruit, squashes and radishes, coconuts and coffee, and pepper and macadamia nuts. Are you getting hungry yet?

WHERE?
India, Southeast Asia

SIZE
0.7–0.8 inch
(17–20 mm) long

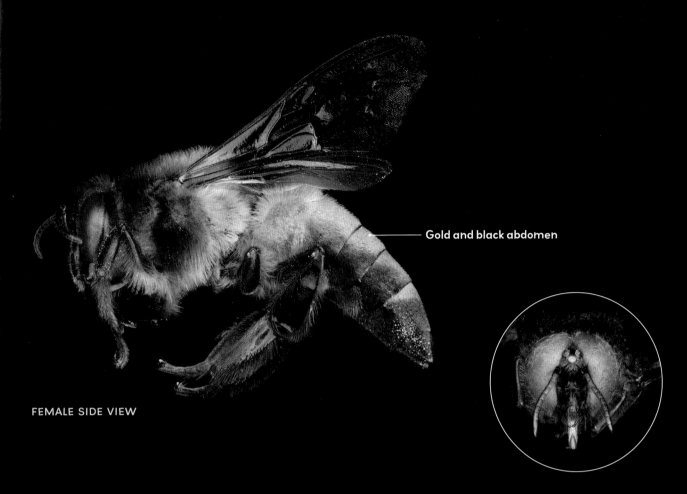

Gold and black abdomen

FEMALE SIDE VIEW

MALE FACE

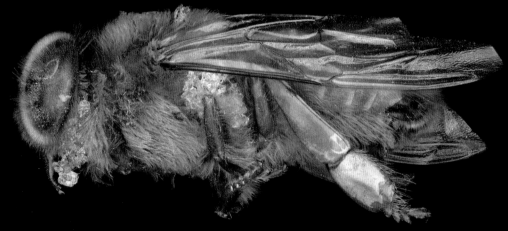

MALE SIDE VIEW

▲ *Apis dorsata is huge and hairy. Note the bulging compound eye of the male (bottom).*

How Honey Happens

Oh, honey. That delicious golden stuff that you drizzle onto breakfast cereal or ice cream. It just makes life sweeter! You might know that bees make honey. But how, exactly, does honey happen?

It starts with a forager bee (see Inside the Hive on page 8 for more on the different roles bees have). Forager bees fly out from the hive to collect nectar, that sugary liquid made by plants, and pollen. When a forager bee finds a delicious flower, it slurps up the nectar with its proboscis and stores it in its *crop*. The crop is a special nectar-holding pocket in the front of the bee's stomach. It allows the bee to drink the nectar but not digest it.

Here's where it gets a little gross. The forager bee, filled with nectar, flies back to the hive and gives it to a waiting worker bee. And how does the forager give it to the worker? It regurgitates it (or throws it up) into the worker bee's mouth. (We warned you.) The worker bee then holds the nectar in its crop until it gets to the honeycomb in the hive. Then the worker bee regurgitates the nectar into the hexagonal shape of the

▼ Apis mellifera *collecting nectar and pollen.*

▼ *Workers regurgitate nectar into honeycomb cells.*

honeycomb. It can take many trips by both forager and worker to fill up one hexagon.

Then the nectar sits in the comb and begins its transformation into honey—a process called *ripening*. Ripening happens thanks to a special substance the bees make in their salivary glands called *invertase* that mixes into the nectar from the worker bee's crop. Invertase breaks the nectar down from liquid that's mostly water to a thick substance that's mostly sugar. The worker bees also buzz their wings over the honeycomb, which makes the water evaporate. Thanks, worker bees!

FLOWERFUL FLAVORS

The taste of honey depends on what types of flowers the forager bees collect nectar from. There's clover honey from clover flowers, and orange blossom honey from orange blossoms. There's even avocado honey, blueberry honey, and dandelion honey.

▼ *Nectar ripens into honey, getting thicker and sweeter over time.*

Himalayan giant honeybee
Apis laboriosa

ID THIS BEE

These huge honeybees have hairy yellow thoraxes with glossy, reddish-black abdomens.

▲ Apis laboriosa *build their nests under cliffs.*

BEE-HAVIOR

Their name says it all, doesn't it? These bees are giant! In fact, they are the biggest honeybees in the world, as far as scientists know.

There is so much that makes these bees special. To start, they live mostly at high altitudes. In the summertime, they build their nests underneath cliffs that are 2,500 to 4,000 meters above sea level. That's between 8,000 and 13,000 feet up in the air! This species is one of the most important pollinators of the Himalayas and other nearby mountain ranges in Asia. These bees visit rhododendron and bottlebrush flowers. They also really like lemon and apple flowers.

In the fall, these giant honeybees start to migrate to lower elevations. It's warmer down there! When food resources dry up in one place, migrating also lets all kinds of animals find food in new places.

An *entomologist* found another reason *Apis laboriosa* might migrate. In Nepal, she watched as giant honeybees were attacked by giant hornets that wanted to eat them. The attacks made the bees drop their pollen, which hit the hornets like weapons. The bees also hissed and shook their bodies to scare off the hornets. But the attacks were constant. The entomologist thought the bees migrated to flee the hornet attacks. Smart move, bees!

WHERE?

The Himalayas of Nepal,

SIZE

1.2 inch (30.5 mm) long

THREATENED!

Declining in Vietnam

FEMALE SIDE VIEW

Hind legs

FEMALE FACE

▲ *These bees have hairy yellow thoraxes and glossy abdomens.*

Black dwarf honeybee *Apis andreniformis*
and red dwarf honeybee *Apis florea*
These two species = subgenus *Micrapis* (all the dwarf honeybees)

STICKY BUSINESS

These skinny little bees are generalists. They visit many different kinds of flowers, such as onion and palm flowers. They make their nests the same way their giant honeybee cousins do. They build a single small piece of honeycomb around a tree branch, then rest on the outside to protect its contents. And they have another special trick: They spread sticky propolis on the branch all around the nest. Nope, it's not to "glue" the hive together or fill up cracks. The propolis keeps out ants that want to steal their honey.

It might not surprise you to learn that these very small bees make a very small amount of honey. Black dwarf honeybees are also very aggressive about defending their hives. (Red dwarf honeybees are gentler.) It is not worth all their stings for a human honey harvester to bother them.

ID THIS BEE

The black dwarf honeybee is black with thin white stripes. The red dwarf honeybee has a fuzzy gray thorax. Its abdomen is reddish black, with white stripes and a thick gold band. These two bees are close relatives. They have a lot in common, looks-wise. In fact, they are often mistaken for each other.

BEE-HAVIOR

The black dwarf honeybee hangs out at high altitudes in the rainy season. It migrates to lower altitudes in the dry season. It is the smallest of all honeybees. The red dwarf honeybee isn't much bigger. It is about a half a millimeter longer. Both these bee species are very common in Asia and Australia. Both species live in colonies just like other honeybees, except their colonies have only a few thousand bees in them. Everything about these bees is littler in every way.

WHERE?
Eastern foothills of Himalayas to Cambodia, Vietnam, Laos, Philippines/Sri Lanka; southern India, Iran, Oman, Pakistan, Thailand

SIZE
Black dwarf honeybee: 0.25–0.4 inch (6.5–10 mm) long

Red dwarf honeybee: 0.3–0.4 inch (7–10 mm) long

THREATENED!
Declining in Vietnam

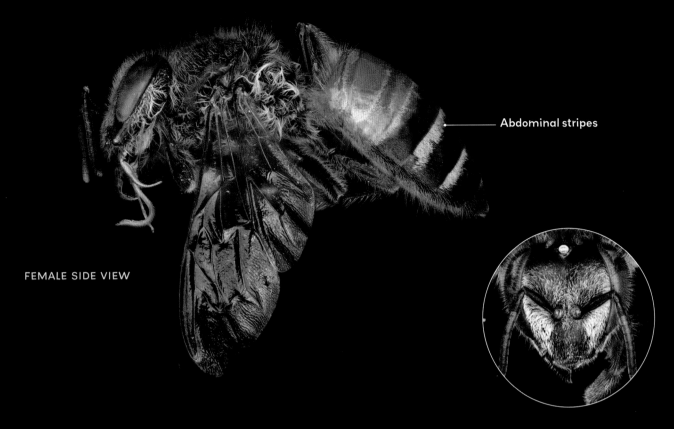

FEMALE SIDE VIEW

Abdominal stripes

FEMALE FACE

MALE SIDE VIEW

▲ *An* Apis florea *female (top) with her iridescent wings, and a male, with his paler coloring and huge compound eye.*

BEHIND THE VEIL:
All about Beekeeping

People figured out that bees make delicious honey thousands of years ago. In fact, ancient rock paintings show people collecting honey from wild bees more than 10,000 years ago. But beekeeping—humans owning and caring for bee colonies—dates back to at least ancient Egypt, some 4,500 years ago.

Today, a person who keeps bees is called a *beekeeper* or an *apiarist*. And hives are kept in an *apiary*, or bee yard.

Beekeepers have one main job: keep the bee colonies living in their hives happy and healthy. To do this, beekeepers regularly inspect the hives for any signs of problems. If they notice any mites, parasites, or other pests invading the hives, they'll treat them to get rid of the problem. If something happens to the queen bee, the beekeeper will ensure the hive makes a new one or, if not, provide the hive with another queen. Beekeepers also help feed bees if pollen or nectar is scarce.

TOOLS OF THE TRADE

Veil: The hat and veil protect the beekeeper's head and face from any startled bees that might sting the apiarist.

Suit: Suit up! Beekeeping suits cover the apiarist's body and prevent stings.

Smoker: With a little bit of fuel, such as dry hay, and some fire, these canisters gently squeeze out smoke. The smoke helps keep the bees focused on their hives instead of the beekeeper.

Hive box: This human-made box helps bees create their layered hives. Inside, the box is lined with frames on which the bees build their honeycombs, lay eggs, care for babies, and store honey. They nest in the center frames and store honey in the outer ones.

Hive tool: This tool, with a flat end and a hooked end, helps the beekeeper pry frames out of the hive box.

▼ A smoker helps calm honeybees so a beekeeper can remove frames full of honey.

Smoker

Hive tool

BUMBLEBEES

Family: Apidae
Genus: *Bombus*

There are 250 species of bumblebees around the world. Mostly they live in the Northern Hemisphere. About 50 species are native to North America, but the majority of them live in Europe and Asia. They tend to prefer to live in the mountains. But you can also find these plump, fuzzy bees in deserts and tundra and forests. They are generalists and *forage* in many different types of flowers. Some of these flowers are very deep. To get to their nectar, some bumblebees have very long tongues.

Many bumblebees don't mind flying in chilly temperatures. They are covered in hair to keep them warm, and they can also make their own heat by shivering their muscles. But they do not make much honey. Pollen and nectar are their main foods.

However, they are excellent pollinators. They use *buzz pollination* when they visit flowers. They vibrate their bodies to loosen the tiny yellow grains. In this way, they can collect lots of pollen and move it between many flowers. Buzz pollination by bumblebees results in more and bigger fruits than *pollination* by honeybees.

Another cool thing bumblebees do is called *trapline foraging*. They visit the same patches of flowers over and over in the same order day after day. This means they might have to fly shorter distances to collect pollen, saving them energy.

Bumblebees are social insects that live in very small colonies in the ground. The *queen* wakes up from *hibernation* in the spring. She builds a hive, then lays all the eggs for her colony inside. First come female workers, then male drones, and finally, new queens. The queen lives for a year. Her workers live for a few weeks. Her drones hatch, mate, and then die.

◀ *A bumblebee visits a globe thistle flower.*

Common eastern bumblebee
Bombus impatiens

ID THIS BEE

Is this the most adorable bee? Its cheerful colors and chubby body make it a top contestant. This is an easy-to-find bumblebee that is black and has a yellow thorax.

BOXES AND BEYOND

Bombus impatiens bees are not picky about the plants they visit. That makes them popular with farmers. Farmers can buy boxes filled with these bees, which were raised in labs. They set the boxes in their fields or their greenhouses. But there's a problem. Eastern bumblebees are sent to farms all over. Sometimes these places are outside their native range, which means they aren't well adapted to life there. They get sick with new diseases that can be passed on to other bees, causing native colonies to collapse. Some people think we should not use eastern bumblebees outside their home habitat.

BEE-HAVIOR

Bombus impatiens has a neat name. *Bombus* is the Greek word for "buzzing sound." BZZZZ! The name *impatiens* may come from the name of one of the flowers these bees visit. But some people think it means these bumblebees are impatient to sting you if you annoy them (they aren't).

Common eastern bumblebees are native to forests and fields. They live in parks and cities. They visit many kinds of plants. Rosemary and chives, tomatoes and blueberries, and cucumbers and cherries are some of their favorites. With their hairy bodies, pollen sticks all over them.

A future bumblebee queen is called a *gyne*. She is born in the fall. Right away, she mates with male bees, and then she hibernates. When she wakes up in early spring, it's time to set up her colony. She is hungry, so she gobbles nectar. Then she finds a mouse or chipmunk hole.

Inside the hole, the queen builds a "honeypot" to store nectar and pollen. She lays eggs on it. Then she sits on the eggs. She repeats this all summer long, growing her colony to between 200 and 1,000 females. Smaller worker bees hang out in the middle of the nest. They feed larvae and tidy up. Bigger bees hang out on the edges. They guard the nest and go out to forage.

The queen makes male bees at the end of summer. She makes new gynes last, before she dies.

WHERE?
Eastern North America

SIZE
Female worker: 0.3–0.6 inch (8.5–16 mm) long

Queen: 0.7–0.8 inch (17–21 mm) long

Male drone: 0.5–0.7 inch (12–17 mm) long

Wings

FEMALE SIDE VIEW

FEMALE FACE

▲ *A queen* Bombus impatiens. *Two sets of powerful wings help get her off the ground. .*

Confusing bumblebee
Bombus perplexus

WATCH YOUR STEP

From April until September, you can find these bees buzzing around forests, wetlands, and orchards. They are common in the midwestern United States, but their range extends from Alaska to Maine. They live as far south as Georgia. These bees love blueberries, blackberries, and apples (who doesn't?) and also rhododendrons, hydrangeas, and clover.

Sometimes queens build their nests in hollow logs. Sometimes they build them right on the ground. Careful where you step!

ID THIS BEE

Another "cutest bee" contestant! Males have a bright lemon-yellow mustache right in the middle of their faces. Females sport handy pollen baskets on their back legs. Females have 12 antennae segments (rather than the 13 for males) and are only yellow on their first and second abdominal sections. Meanwhile, males are yellow almost everywhere on their heads and bodies.

▲ Bombus perplexus *gathers pollen.*

BEE-HAVIOR

These shaggy gals and guys are pretty rare. That means scientists have not had much chance to study them. Which makes it hard for them to tell these bees from other similar-colored bees that live in the same places—bumblebees like *Bombus vagans*, *Bombus sandersoni*, and *Bombus bimaculatus*.

WHERE?
Northern North America

SIZE
Females and males:
0.3–0.5 inch
(7.5–13 mm) long

Queens: 0.75–1 inch
(19–25 mm) long

THREATENED!
Special concern in Wisconsin

Wings

MALE SIDE VIEW

MALE FACE

FEMALE FACE

FEMALE SIDE VIEW

▲ *You can tell a male (top) from a female (bottom) Bombus perplexus by his 13 rather than 12 antennae segments. The female has pollen baskets on her back legs.*

Tricolored bumblebee
(also known as *orange-belted bumblebee*)

Bombus ternarius

SPECIAL FEATURES

Entomologists say *Bombus ternarius* bees have short hair and a short tongue. The flowers they like to visit are shallow rather than deep—they do not have to slurp far to get the tasty nectar they crave.

Like honeybee workers, *Bombus ternarius* workers have stingers. They use them to protect their nests and themselves. But bumblebee stingers have no barbs. That means the workers can pull them out and sting again. This is different from honeybee stingers. Those are barbed, so they stay in their victims. When a honeybee pulls away, the stinger pulls out of its body, and the bee doesn't survive. *Bombus ternarius* is very gentle, though. This bee will only sting if it is threatened. It does not have ears to hear you coming. But it can feel your movement.

ID THIS BEE

Unlike the confusing bumblebee, the tricolored bumblebee is not very confusing at all. That is thanks to its three (tri-) distinct colors. It has a yellow thorax. Its abdomen is first yellow, then orange with black stripes. And it has a black T between its wings. It is a very dashing-looking bumblebee.

BEE-HAVIOR

Wisconsin is known for its cranberry marshes. Many of the cranberries you eat at Thanksgiving or drink as juice are raised there. What makes cranberries grow so well? Good pollinators like this bulky bumblebee.

These bumblebees are very common in their native range. They like wetlands and woodlands. And they appreciate a tasty blueberry or raspberry flower in addition to cranberries. To find *Bombus ternarius*, try looking in patches of wild goldenrod that grow in late summer. They nest in thick stands of this plant.

WHERE?

Northeastern United States, Canada

SIZE

Female: 0.3–0.5 inch (8–13 mm) long

Queen: 0.67–0.75 inch (17–19 mm) long

Male: 0.4–0.5 inch (9.5–13 mm) long

▼ *A female* Bombus ternarius *seen from the side, and from above. Her orange butt is a useful ID tool!*

Fuzzy abdomen

FEMALE SIDE VIEW

FEMALE FACE

FEMALE TOP VIEW

Bumblebee Aerodynamics

The mystery started in the 1930s. French scientist August Magnan inspected a bumblebee. He took in its big round body and its tiny wings, then considered the physics of flight. *There's no way this bee should be able to fly*, he thought. And so, for decades, how bumblebees managed to buzz around was a mystery.

All that changed thanks to a series of tests scientists performed in the early 2000s. In one study using a robotic bee wing, scientists discovered that instead of flapping their wings up and down, bumblebees actually flap them back and forth. Turns out, this discovery solves the mystery of bumblebee flight. By flapping their wings back and forth, bumblebees create tiny swirls of air. The currents from these swirls help lift the big bumblebee body up and up. In another study that put actual bumblebees in a wind tunnel and filmed them flying, scientists realized that bumblebee wings don't flap in sync. Each flaps on its own. This doesn't make them the most efficient fliers—in fact, you could say they're a bit bumbling—but they manage to get off the ground just fine!

▶ *Bumblebees actually flap their wings back and forth rather than up and down.*

▼ *Coming in for a landing on a foxglove flower.*

Rusty patched bumblebee
Bombus affinis

ENDANGERED

Now *Bombus affini*s is hard to find. Its population has declined by almost 90 percent in its normal range. There are not many bumblebees in worse shape in the United States. (*Bombus franklini* comes close. It is also classified as critically endangered.)

Scientists still hope that humans can save these bumblebees. Listing them on endangered species lists shows people they are in trouble. It also means there are laws to protect them now. In the meantime, scientists are working to bring back bumblebee habitat. They are teaching farmers ways they can help, such as planting native species and leaving grasses unmowed.

ID THIS BEE

If you can find this bumblebee, you will see that it is yellow with a black head and backside. It also has a rusty patch on its second abdominal segment. Now you know how it got its name. The queen has no patch, though.

BEE-HAVIOR

These are big bees with short tongues. They have a lot of the same habits as other bumblebees. Or rather, they *did*. Once upon a time, rusty patched bumblebees were found in 29 US states and in Canada. They buzzed around grasslands and prairies and marshes and woodlands. They foraged in clover, goldenrod, sunflowers, and even wild blueberries and cranberries. Workers didn't fly more than half a mile from their nests. They didn't have to. In very early spring and very late fall, and all the time in between, they could find many different kinds of flowers to feed them.

Then life got hard for *Bombus affinis*. People started building on grasslands and prairies. Flowers disappeared. People started turning wildland into huge farms. They sprayed chemicals on their crops. Some farmers brought in honeybees and *Bombus impatiens* and other bees to pollinate their plants. Those other bees competed with *Bombus affinis* for food. And they spread their diseases.

WHERE?
Eastern and midwestern United States; Ontario and Quebec, Canada

SIZE
Female worker: 0.4–0.63 inch (10–16 mm) long

Queen: 0.8–0.9 inch (20–22 mm) long

THREATENED!
Critically endangered

MALE SIDE VIEW

Rusty patch

QUEEN FACE

FEMALE TOP VIEW

▲ *The now-rare* Bombus affinis *male (top) and female (bottom).*

Red-shanked carder bee
Bombus ruderarius

ID THIS BEE
This is a species of bumblebee. A clue is that the first part of its Latin name is the word *Bombus*. Females are mostly black, with some red hairs and a ruddy backside. Males have grayish-yellow bands on their abdomens.

SNEAK ATTACK
Sometimes other babies are feeding inside a *Bombus ruderarius* nest. *Bombus campestris* is a cuckoo bumblebee. Cuckoo bees are parasites that lay their eggs in someone else's nest. That way, someone else takes care of its babies. For *Bombus campestris*, that someone else is *Bombus ruderarius*.

BEE-HAVIOR
This bee used to be found in many places in the United Kingdom and across Europe. But scientists say it is in *catastrophic* decline in the United Kingdom, which means the number of red-shanked carder bees there is dropping fast. Its populations in Europe are dropping too.

Bombus ruderarius is easier to find in grasslands and other still-wild places. Places like wetlands, marshes, and dunes near the sea. Places where people have not made roads or built houses. Wild places still have plenty of the food that *Bombus ruderarius* needs. Mint and pea and figwort flowers are some favorites. *Bombus ruderarius* collects pollen from their flowers. For nectar, it visits different plants, such as red clover, common vetch, and thistle. These all have deep flowers. That makes the long tongue of *Bombus ruderarius* just right for collecting their nectar.

Queens build their nests on the ground or near the top of mouse burrows. They look for sites in tall grasses near moss. They use those materials to build nests that are just right for raising baby bees. *Bombus ruderarius* raises colonies of only 20 to 50 workers. In addition to being a bumblebee, *Bombus ruderarius* is a carder bee. Carder bees are "pocket makers." Workers make pockets in the sides of nest cells. They fill the pockets with pollen. This way, baby bee larvae can feed themselves. It's a good trick for tired babysitters!

WHERE?
Europe, northeast Asia (United Kingdom to Siberia)

SIZE
Female: 0.6 inch (15 mm) long

Queen: 0.67 inch (17 mm) long

Male: 0.5 inch (13 mm) long

THREATENED!
Declining

Mostly black

FEMALE SIDE VIEW

FEMALE FACE

MALE SIDE VIEW

▲ *Females (top) are almost all black. Males are grayish yellow on their abdomens.*

A BEE-AUTIFUL GARDEN:
Plant Flowers to Attract Pollinators

You've probably figured it out by now: bees are important pollinators that keep plants and crops around the world buzzing! You can help them out by creating a garden perfect for pollinators. Here's how!

The first step is selecting where you'll plant your garden. Bees prefer sunny spots to shady ones, so look for an area that gets good sunlight for most of the day. They also don't like windy areas.

Next, pick your plants. Not just any plants will do, though. Ideally, you'll want to select flowering plants native to your area. Native plants will survive best in your habitat and will attract native bees. For help figuring out what plants are native, visit your local arboretum, botanical society, or garden center. Look for perennials—plants that will come back each year after winter.

You know by now that bees like plenty of pollen and nectar, so look for flowering plants. And make sure to select a variety of sizes and shapes. As you've seen in this book, bees come in many shapes and sizes, so having big flowers and little flowers, as well as deep flowers and shallow flowers, will make sure you've got a flower for every bee species near you. Color matters too! Bees tend to visit flowers that are violet, blue, purple, yellow, and white. Make sure to have a good mix.

Now you're ready to plant! When putting your pollinator-friendly plants in the ground, make sure to arrange them together in clumps rather than spread out around a garden. Clumps give bees a bunch of flowers to land on with little moving around, rather than having to buzz along to find their next stop.

▶ *A field of wildflowers is a sure way to attract bees and other important pollinators.*

GROW A POLLINATOR-FRIENDLY GARDEN

Some plants bees particularly like are:

Aster
Bee balm (wild bergamot)
Black-eyed Susan
Borage
Cotoneaster
Currant
Globe thistle
Goldenrod
Huckleberry
Hyssop
Liatris
Lupine
Marjoram
Mint
Pansy
Purple coneflower
Rhododendron
Rosemary
Sage
Wild lilac
Zinnia

Some they *don't* like are:

Eucalyptus
Ferns
Lemongrass

WHAT YOU CAN DO

Avoid pesticides and chemicals in your garden. Both harm bees, even if you don't intend them to. If you have a pest problem, look for an organic or nontoxic solution instead. Don't spray chemicals on your lawn. Plant it with grasses that do not need mowing. Plant a fruit tree, such as a plum tree. *Bombus affinis* loves plum flowers! Plant lots of lupines, asters, and bee balm. Ask your friends and neighbors to do these things too.

CUCKOO BEES

Families in North America: Apidae, Halictidae, Megachilidae
Genus: *Apidae*

There are many kinds of cuckoo bees, classified into three different families. And there are a lot of names for them. They are known as *kleptoparasites*. *Klepto* means "thief" in Greek. A *parasite* is an animal that lives off a host animal. Cuckoo bees are also known as *pollen thieves* because they steal pollen from other bees' babies rather than collecting it themselves. And, of course, they are known as *cuckoo bees*. That is because their behavior is similar to that of birds called *cuckoos*. Cuckoo birds lay their eggs in other birds' nests. Cuckoo bees do the same thing, but they lay their eggs in other bees' nests.

Cuckoo bees differ depending on what family they are from. Cuckoos in the Apidae and Halictidae families are smooth rather than hairy. This is because they don't collect pollen. They range in size from very tiny to large, and they look like wasps. They are parasites of bees that nest mostly in the ground. You can find them hovering low, looking for nests to break into.

Megachilidae cuckoos look more like bees. They are parasites of bees that nest on twigs and in wood.

All cuckoos are solitary bees. They mostly work the same way. They sneak into other bee nests and lay eggs there. This way they pass on all the work of building nests, collecting food, and raising babies. When cuckoo bee larvae hatch, they often kill the host bee larvae with their huge jaws. Then they eat the pollen in the nest cells.

There are far fewer parasitic bees than host bees. Too many parasitic bees would make the host bees extinct. Then who would raise the parasitic bee babies?

◄ *Cuckoo bees are common in the bee world.*

Neon cuckoo bee *Thyreus nitidulus*
and blue-banded bee *Amegilla cingulata*

ID THIS BEE

This cuckoo bee species lives up to its "neon" name. It is bright blue with black stripes. Its Latin name means "a little shiny." And that seems just right too. *Amegilla cingulata* is a species of blue-banded bee that has blue bands on its abdomen and a fuzzy yellow thorax.

CRAZY FOR NECTAR

What does a neon cuckoo bee do with all its spare time? It forages in flowers. But it doesn't like pollen. It forages for nectar only. It is a generalist, but its favorite nectar is from Brazilian button flowers. Its iridescent sheen is common in the insect world. It comes from having an exoskeleton made up of layers. Those layers reflect sunlight.

BEE-HAVIOR

If you're a solitary female bee, you live a pretty busy life. A lot of your time is spent building your nest. More time is spent making babies. A lot of time is spent foraging for food. Wouldn't it be nice if there was a way to make things a little easier for yourself? If you are a neon cuckoo bee, you have figured out a way. You've discovered how to make your neighbor do a lot of your hard work. That neighbor is a species of blue-banded bee called *Amegilla cingulata*.

Blue-banded bees are some of the most important pollinators in Australia. More than one-third of crops happen because of them—crops like tomatoes, eggplants, and peppers. Blue-banded bees use buzz pollination like bumblebees do. Only their technique is different. They bang their heads inside a flower 350 times per second! This makes the pollen fall onto their heads and bodies.

The blue-banded queen bee makes her nest in burrows. The neon cuckoo queen bee sneaks on in there. She lays her eggs in empty brood cells when no one is looking. The clueless blue-banded queen bee lays her eggs in the cells too. She places balls of pollen and nectar with the eggs, then seals the cells up with wax. A few weeks later, the cuckoo bees hatch and eat all the food that the blue-banded bee left for her own babies.

WHERE?
Australia, Papua New Guinea

SIZE
Neon cuckoo bee:
0.4–0.5 inch
(10–13 mm) long

Blue-banded bee:
0.4–0.47 inch
(10–12 mm) long

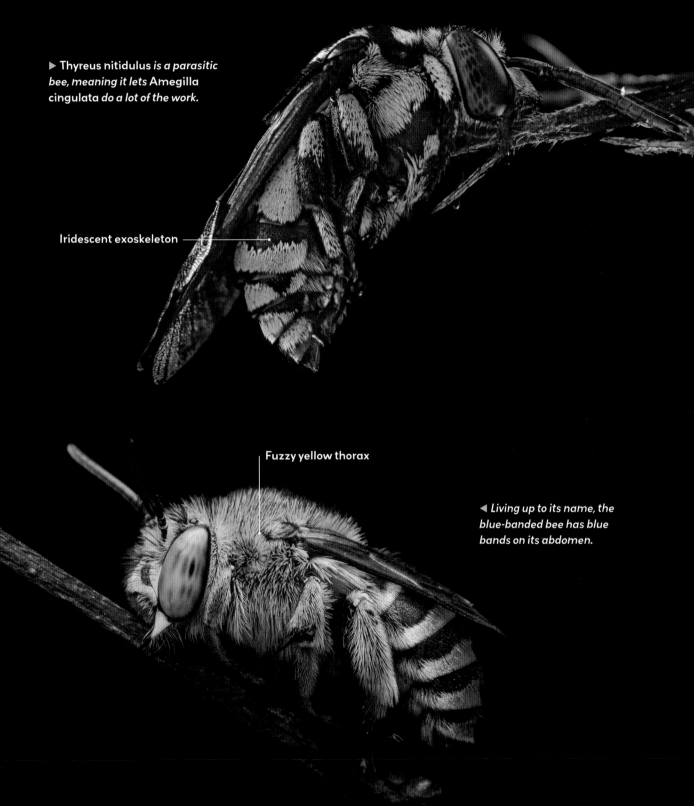

▶ **Thyreus nitidulus** *is a parasitic bee, meaning it lets* **Amegilla cingulata** *do a lot of the work.*

Iridescent exoskeleton

Fuzzy yellow thorax

◀ *Living up to its name, the blue-banded bee has blue bands on its abdomen.*

Macropis cuckoo bee *Epeoloides pilosula*
and four *Macropis* species

OIL BEES

You might think life is smooth sailing when you are a parasite—you rely on your hosts to do all the work! But *Epeoloides pilosula* bees depend on other bees to survive, and those bees they depend on are also pretty rare. They are four species of *Macropis* oil bees, and they are the most ancient of all the bees; they evolved on our planet a long time ago. They collect pollen and floral oils from one kind of plant only. That plant is called loosestrife. The bees carry loosestrife oil to their nests in special pockets on their legs. They use it as food and also to make their nests waterproof.

ID THIS BEE

This cuckoo bee is smooth, mostly black, and wasplike. Its body sections are slim and very distinct from each other. *Macropis* oil bees are medium size and black in color.

BEE-HAVIOR

One-fifth of native bees in the United States don't collect any pollen. Remember neon cuckoo bees? They sneak into other bees' nests and lay their eggs there. And when the larvae hatch, they gobble the host bees' pollen. The grown bees live on nectar.

There are about 70 species of *Epeolus* bees in North America. They are pretty chonky, and most of them have hairy black-and-white stripes on their abdomens. But the *Macropis* cuckoo bee, *Epeoloides pilosula*, is all black. It is also not an

Epeolus cuckoo bee. *Epeoloides* means "*Epeolus* look-alike." There are only two known species of *Epeoloides* bees. *Epeoloides pilosula* lives in North America. The other one lives in Europe.

Epeoloides pilosula used to have a range across the eastern United States. That changed, though. Scientists thought they were extinct until 2002. Then they found two of the bees in Nova Scotia, Canada. So now we know they're not extinct. We also know that they are one of the rarest bees on the North American continent.

WHERE?
Eastern North America

SIZE
Macropis cuckoo bee:
Female worker:
0.4–0.63 inch
(10–16 mm) long

Queen: 0.8–0.9 inch
(20–22 mm) long

Male drone: 0.5–0.7 inch
(13–17.5 mm) long

Macropis: Up to 0.6 inch
(15 mm) long

THREATENED!
Endangered in Connecticut and Canada; three species declining and/or threatened

Hind legs

MALE SIDE VIEW

MALE FACE

▲ *A male* Macropis *cuckoo bee. Can you see its very distinct body sections?*

MASON BEES

Family: Megachilidae
Genus: *Osmia*

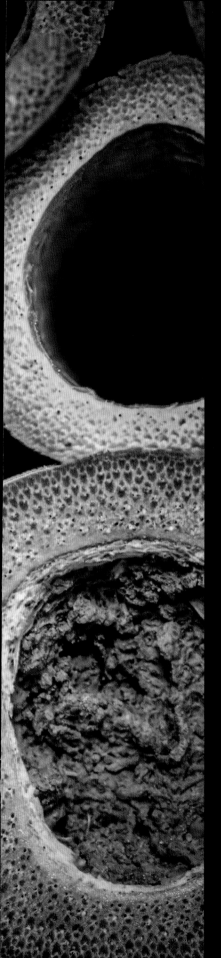

Worldwide, there are about 500 species of these colorful, stocky bees. They are usually shades of bright blue or metallic green. More than 130 species are native to North America. They like to live high up in the mountains or low down at sea level. Many of them really, really like to pollinate orchard fruits. We bet you guessed that this makes them farmer favorites.

Osmia means "odor" in Greek. These bees got their name because they mark their hives with an odor that smells like lemons. Every bee has its own very special lemony odor, though. That way, each one can sniff out its own nest.

Mason bees are solitary. They make their nests in all kinds of holes and cracks and crevices. Some of them use hollow twigs or reeds. Like human masons who make walls out of bricks and cement, mason bees use mud to make nest cells. They scoop mud up in their jaws and mix it with mashed-up leaves and tree sap.

These bees are mostly generalists. But a few mason bees are specialists. Each species has its own hairs on its head and body for collecting pollen from different kinds of flowers. Females have a special body part called a crop in the front of their stomachs. Remember how they store nectar in it to feed to their babies?

◄ Osmia bicornis *emerging from nest tubes in an insect hotel.*

Blue orchard bee

Osmia lignaria

ID THIS BEE

Blue orchard bees are a species of mason bee. They are also known as *BOBs*. They have metallic blue coloring, fuzzy black bodies, and long antennae. If they buzz by quickly, you might confuse them for a fly!

FARMER BOBS

Solitary bees may be common, but BOBs are special in their own way. Even in chilly early spring, they visit flowers in orchards. Fruit farmers love BOBs because they do the work of pollinating when honeybees and bumblebees are still huddled up. (They're also really good at it, "swimming" across flowers to catch pollen on their bellies.) Bee ranchers raise BOBs by getting them to nest in tubes. They store BOB cocoons until apple and cherry trees bloom. Then they sell them to farmers to hatch out in their orchards.

BEE-HAVIOR

Imagine spending your whole grown-up life alone. Does it sound, well, lonely? In fact, that's just the way things are for about 90 percent of all bees. They're solitary.

A BOB's first job is to mate. Afterward, a female finds a hole in a log or other wood to lay her eggs in. She wants to make this hole cozy. So she uses mud to make nest cells. Out in a field, she rolls mud into balls. Then she flies the balls home, one at a time. How? She tucks them into the space between her mouthparts and front legs.

She also collects nectar and pollen. This is food for her future babies. She might have to visit flowers 30,000 times to gather enough. She kneads up pollen and nectar into a ball and puts it in the first nest cell. She lays a tiny egg on the ball. She seals the cell up with more mud. She builds five nest cells or more. When she's done, a mother BOB is exhausted, and her wings are ragged. No wonder she only lives for 20 days.

The BOB larvae hatch. They munch pollen balls as they grow through five stages called *instars*. They spin themselves into cocoons. Inside, they transform into grown bees. When spring arrives, they push out of their cells. Male cells are at the front of the nest, so they emerge first. They wait outside to mate with newborn female BOBs. Males die a few days later.

WHERE?
United States, Canada

SIZE
Female: 0.55 inch (14 mm)

Male: 0.43 inch

FEMALE SIDE VIEW

The female is bigger
than the male

FEMALE FACE

Long antennae

12 body segments

MALE SIDE VIEW

▲ *Female (top) or male (bottom),
you can tell these are BOBs by
their metallic blue bodies.*

Snail shell bee
Osmia bicolor

ID THIS BEE

This small, hairy mason bee has a black head and thorax. Its abdomen is bright orange with thin black stripes. Males are a little less bright.

▲ *Snail shell bees lay their eggs in . . . you guessed it, snail shells.*

BEE-HAVIOR

Looking for super-cool bee behavior? Then *Osmia bicolor* is your species. Notice its English name. "Snail shell bee" refers to the fact that this little insect makes its nests in snail shells.

Here's how it happens: A garden snail outgrows its shell and leaves it empty. The bee finds it lying in the grass. She twirls it until its opening is facing away from the sky. She does not want any rain getting in.

Next, she makes a protective barrier of munched-up leaves. She chews up a nectar and pollen ball and places it inside the shell. On it, she lays an egg. Then she seals up the shell's opening with sand, bits of broken shell, and pieces of bark. She may partly bury the shell in the dirt. Then she flies off to bring back twigs and moss and grass. She makes these into a covering for the shell. She repeats this whole process with six or seven shells.

When the babies hatch, it is still late winter. The males live for a few days—just long enough to mate. The females spend the spring visiting flowers like bluebells, dandelions, and daisies.

WHERE?
Europe to western Asia

SIZE
0.47 inch (12 mm) long

THREATENED!
Nationally scarce in Britain

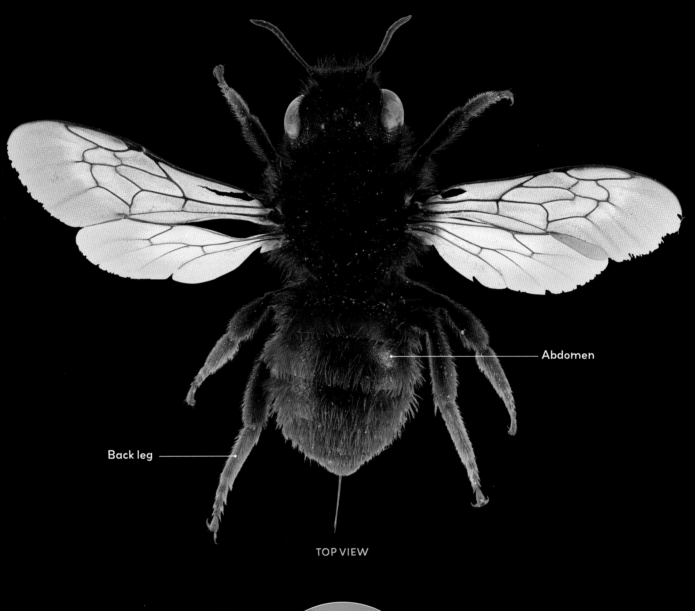

Abdomen

Back leg

TOP VIEW

FEMALE FACE

▲ Osmia bicolor *has a hairy black head and a bright orange-striped thorax.*

◄ *Her fuzzy head is good at collecting pollen.*

Bees at a Glance

One way scientists can tell one species of bee from another is by examining differences in their bodies. Let's examine a bee and learn the names of its body parts.

BASIC BEE BODY

Every bee body is made up of these parts:

Wings (two pairs)

Head

Exoskeleton

Abdomen

Legs (three pairs)

SIDE VIEW

A CLOSER LOOK

Compound eye: Bees have two sets of eyes. The compound eye has tons of ommatidia, which sense light.
Ocelli: Bees use this set of three simple eyes to pick up movement.
Mandibles: Tough mouthparts that chomp like jaws.
Proboscis: This mouthpart acts like a straw for fluids.
Antennae: Bees can pick up smells and air movements with their antennae.

FACE

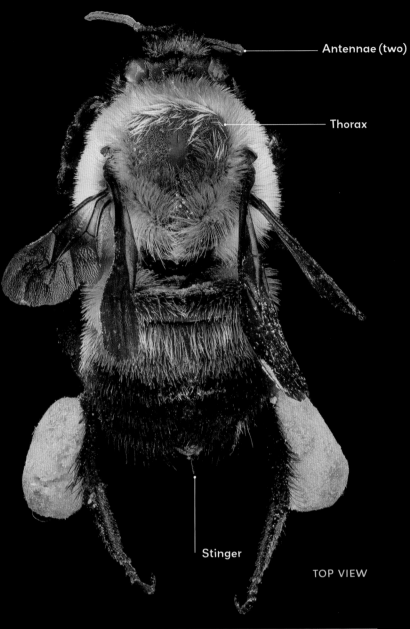

Antennae (two)

Thorax

Stinger

TOP VIEW

BEYOND BASICS

Forewings: These wings come *before* the hind wings.

Hind wings: These are the wings closest to the bee's abdomen.

Forelegs: These are the bee's front-most pair of legs.

Antennae cleaners: Each foreleg has special hairs that help bees clean their antennae.

Middle legs: These are between the forelegs and hind legs.

Hind legs: These are the bee's backmost legs.

Scopa: This collection of thick hairs helps bees collect pollen.

HONEYBEE

LONG-HORNED BEE

BLUE-BANDED BEE

BEE DIFFERENT

How much can bee bodies vary? They can be tiny or huge, hairy or sleek, bright colored or black all over. Look at the differences between a western honeybee, a long-horned bee, and a blue-banded bee.

Horn-faced bee
Osmia cornifrons

ID THIS BEE

These little mason bees are fuzzy all over. Their flat black color has a coppery glow. Females have yellow hairs on the thorax. They all have short, thick horns on their lower faces. You have to look close to see them.

▲ Osmia cornifrons *leaves its nest.*

BEE-HAVIOR

Horn-faced bees are solitary, like all mason bees. They make their nests in hollow stems and holes in trees made by other bugs. Sometimes they prefer cracks in rocks or bark for laying their eggs.

Osmia cornifrons is another species that's great at pollination. These bees hatch in April and die by June, overlapping with pollination seasons for many plants. Both males and females visit flowers. They are used all over Japan and Korea for pollinating apples. These bees were brought to the United States in the 1970s to do this job. In the United States, they are used to pollinate apples and also peaches, pears, cherries, and other fruits.

Some people think this is great because each one of these bees can pollinate 2,500 flowers a day. Some people think this is a mistake. They wonder why fruit farmers don't use BOBs instead. BOBs are native to the United States and are also very good pollinators. They do not compete with native bees or spread diseases when they are in their natural range.

Japanese horn-faced bees have now settled on the East Coast. Scientists worry that they may be making other bees sick. Do we need these bees for our crops? Or do they cause more problems than they solve?

WHERE?
East Asia, US East Coast and Midwest

SIZE
Female: 0.3–0.47 inch (8–12 mm) long
Male: 0.3–0.4 inch (8–10 mm) long

◀ *Note the pale hair of the male (top) and the coppery sheen of the female (bottom).*

MALE FACE

Thorax segment

FEMALE SIDE VIEW

Blueberry bee
Osmia ribifloris

BEE-HAVIOR

Did you guess that this bee's name comes from how much it likes to visit blueberry flowers? *Osmia ribifloris* is an important pollinator of these little blue fruits. It is even better than honeybees at getting lots and lots of blueberries to grow. Is it a coincidence that it is the same color as its favorite fruit? Scientists have noticed that many blue-colored bees are fans of flowers of blue-colored fruits.

These bees land on flowers with all six of their legs. They use their front two legs to pull themselves inside the petals. They stick in their tongues to drink up nectar. At the same time, the bees bang their legs around to get pollen to shake onto them. They wipe the pollen onto the underside of their abdomens. Some of it also sticks to the hairs on a spot on their heads. That spot is called a *safe site*. It is in just the right place to rub that pollen off where it will fertilize a flower.

These small gals and guys like to live in hilly forests. Females use leaves from blueberry bushes and rosebushes to make cells in the nests they build. When males hatch in the spring, they court females by folding their wings and vibrating their bodies to make a buzzing sound.

▲ *The blueberry bee uses its entire body to collect pollen.*

WHERE?
Western United States

SIZE
Female: 0.3–0.47 inch (8–12 mm) long

Male: 0.33–0.44 inch (9–12 mm) long

MALE SIDE VIEW

Males are green

FEMALE SIDE VIEW

Females are blue

▲ *The glittery colors of blueberry bees make them look like flying jewels.*

CARPENTER BEES

Genus: *Xylocopa*

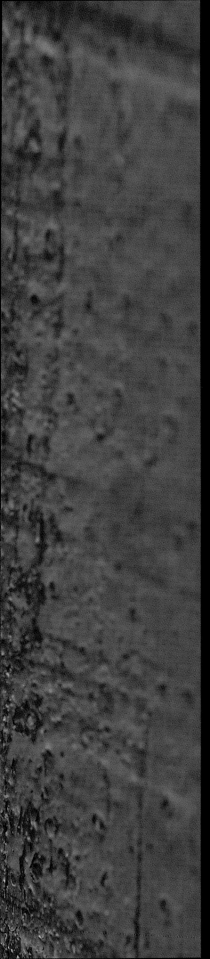

X *ylocopa* is the scientific name of this family. *Xylocopa* means "woodworker" in Greek. Can you guess why the name fits? These very large bees make their homes in pieces of wood. They chew and chew through bark and branches to make holes that they rest and nest in. (Although some carpenter bees prefer to make nests in hollow stems.) They spit the wood out as they go. These nests are called galleries.

Carpenters are solitary bees, but some females like to build their galleries close to each other. They lay a brood, then stick around until the eggs hatch. They also feed their babies until they are grown. These offspring are born in the fall, then hibernate over winter all together in the *gallery* their mother built.

There are 500 species of carpenter bees around the world, and they are mostly tropical bees. They like to live where it is warm and wet. A few of them like to live where it is warm and dry—in deserts.

The bigger the bee, the more pollen it can carry. This is true for carpenter bees. Their big muscular legs are covered with thick hairs called scopa. These hairs help them bring pollen back to their nests. They are generalists and are fond of many kinds of flowers. But they like to visit the same kind of flower day after day when they are building their nests. This is called *flower constancy*. It lets bees pick the flowers that are closest by and most abundant. This saves them time when they are busy getting ready for babies.

Carpenter bees also like nectar. So much that they are nectar hogs. They don't just slurp some nectar and move on. They bite a hole in a flower to get all the nectar out. None left for anyone else!

◀ Xylocopa virginica *making nest hole in a tree.*

Eastern carpenter bee

Xylocopa virginica

ID THIS BEE

Here's a big ol' carpenter bee that has a glossy blackish head and a fuzzy yellow thorax. It has a black dot in the middle of the yellow. Sometimes it is mistaken for a bumblebee.

NOT MUCH OUCH

Female *Xylocopa virginica* bees have stingers. But scientists say they don't use them very much, and when they do, it doesn't really hurt. Males have no stingers. But that doesn't stop them from trying to protect the nest. They fly up close to anyone they think is a predator and buzz very loudly. Would that scare you off?

BEE-HAVIOR

Xylocopa virginica bees like to find a great place to live. Near some pine trees, for example. Or in a wood fence. Or in the side of your wood house. Then they chew some tunnels into the wood to make their nests. Obviously, these bees have big strong jaws. Can you imagine chewing up a house for yourself?

When they find a good neighborhood, they stick around for generations. Every year, newly born bees will tidy up old nests to move into or build new ones nearby. Females mostly like to nest together, with up to five of them sharing the work and the space. Usually, there is one entrance to a group dwelling. Separate tunnels inside lead to individual nests.

Larvae eat nectar and pollen. But young newborn bees only eat nectar. Their moms bring it to them from flowers, such as bluebells, basil, and currants. They use those big jaws to chomp through to the nectar from underneath the flower. This is called *nectar robbing* because it robs the flower of pollination services. It also doesn't leave any nectar for anyone else.

Xylocopa virginica bees do not mate until after they have hibernated for the winter. In fact, newborn females stay in the nest and are fed by older females for the whole summer. They do have one job, and that is guarding the nest. This is the only species of bee that has moms and daughters living together, with only the moms doing almost all the work.

WHERE?

Eastern, central, and southern United States into Guatemala

SIZE

0.75–0.9 inch (19–23 mm) long

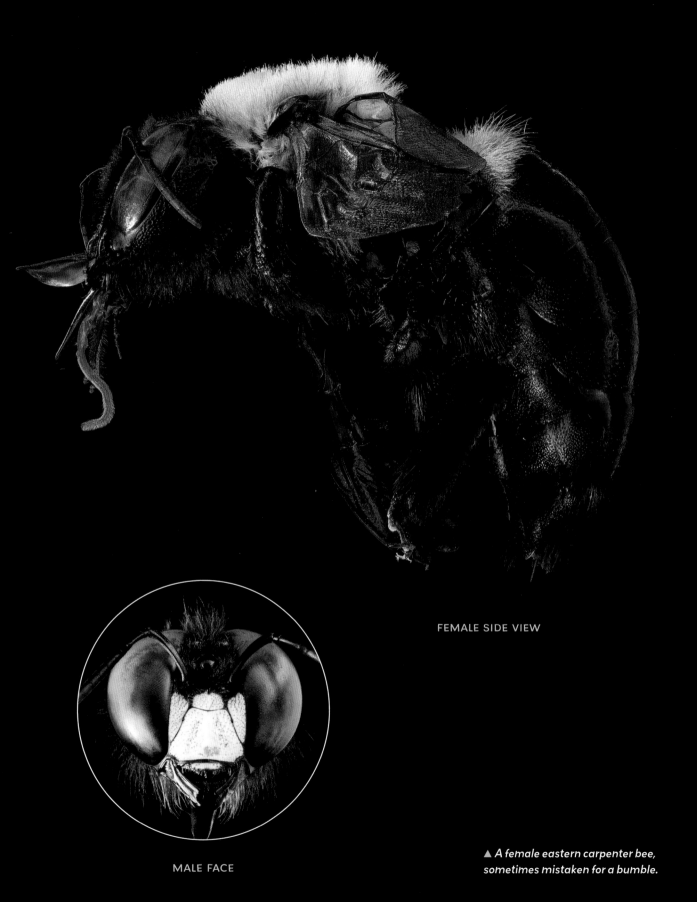

FEMALE SIDE VIEW

MALE FACE

▲ *A female eastern carpenter bee,
sometimes mistaken for a bumble.*

Green carpenter bee

Xylocopa aerata

ON THE BRINK

Xylocopa aerata was once found throughout its native Australia. But bushfires and loss of habitat made it extinct almost everywhere. But thanks to *conservation* efforts, it hung on in certain places.

One of those places is called Kangaroo Island. Part of this island is a refuge—a protected area of land designated for wildlife. But one thing the creatures are not protected from is wildfires. *Climate change* is making wildfires worse, which affects *Xylocopa aerata*, since these bees nest in dead parts of plants. That means their nests burn easily.

In 2007, wildfires burned a lot of Kangaroo Island. But some *Xylocopa aerata* nests remained. The bees made new nests, and scientists helped them by putting out nesting stalks made of balsa wood. By 2020, there were at least 150 nests on Kangaroo Island. Then more wildfires burned every last nest and all the plants the bees use for foraging.

Scientists are working hard to figure out what they can do. Luckily, there are still some bees on the mainland. Maybe scientists can bring some of those bees to Kangaroo Island, and maybe this sad story will have a happy ending one day.

ID THIS BEE

This is one of the largest bees in Australia. It is metallic green and gold in color. It may look purplish or bluish, depending on what angle you see it from. Males have yellow marks on their faces. This is how you can tell them apart from females. They make deep buzzing sounds when they fly. *Xylocopa aerata* is also considered "friendly" and not inclined to sting people.

BEE-HAVIOR

A mother bee hollows out the stalks of special plants called grass trees or in the dead trunks of *Banksia* plants with her powerful jaws, making long tunnels that end in a nest. Sometimes several females use the same nest. This is very convenient. One bee can lay her eggs while the other bees guard the entrance. Over the winter, male and female bees hibernate in the tunnels. In the spring and summer, they buzz-pollinate guinea flowers, velvet bushes, and flax lilies. They are especially important because other types of bees do not pollinate these kinds of flowers.

WHERE?
New South Wales, Australia

SIZE
0.79 inch (20 mm) long

THREATENED!
Declining everywhere except Victoria and mainland South Australia, where they are thought to be extinct.

Metallic abdomen

FEMALE TOP VIEW

MALE TOP VIEW

▲ *The metallic body of the Xylocopa
makes it look almost jewel-like.*

Valley carpenter bee

Xylocopa sonorina & *Xylocopa varipuncta*

ID THIS BEE

When it is found in the United States, the valley carpenter bee is one of the largest bees around. Compared to some of the massive bees found in Asia, though, some people might consider them only medium-size bees. Females are fuzzy black. Their wings have a violet sheen. Males are fuzzy and pale brown with green eyes.

ONE BEE, TWO NAMES

Did you notice that these bees have two different scientific names? Many bees look alike. This means they have sometimes been misidentified. That is especially true for bees that turn up in unexpected places. Entomologists did not expect to find *Xylocopa varipuncta* in Hawaii. Turns out, it hitched a ride from the mainland and became known in the islands as *Xylocopa sonorina*. But DNA tests tell us what we did not know before. *Xylocopa varipuncta* and *Xylocopa sonorina* are one and the same bee.

BEE-HAVIOR

These bees are so big that they can't fit into a lot of flowers. This might help explain why they are nectar thieves; they make a hole in a flower to drink its delicious nectar, rather than going inside the flower. This "robs" the flower of pollination services. Also, their eggs are the biggest of all insect eggs. They are 0.59 inch (15 mm) long! Females lay them in all kinds of interesting woody places, such as inside telephone poles, in outdoor furniture, or in the eaves of your house.

Valley carpenter bees mate in an unusual way. Males gather together in bushes. Then, all at once, they release perfume from glands in their thoraxes. The perfume smells like roses. The female bees smell it and go crazy. They come flying toward the smell, fast. When they get to the bushes, they find no roses. Only male bees. Now they have to decide which of the males to mate with.

Many bee species live for a few weeks or even a year. But these carpenter bees can live up to three years. Females might raise more than one brood each year. That can make for a lot of carpenter bees flying around in the summer. They like to get up early in the morning to forage. And they are not picky about what they eat for breakfast. They are generalists and like all kinds of fruit and vegetable flowers in your garden: tomatoes, eggplants, and plums, to name just a few. They buzz-pollinate these flowers, just like bumblebees do.

WHERE?

Hawaiian Islands, California, Texas, China, Japan, Philippines, Samoa

SIZE

1 inch (25 mm) long

▶ *The valley carpenter bee*

Double-banded carpenter bee
Xylocopa caffra

ID THIS BEE

You'll find this species in countries all over Africa. The female is a fuzzy black color. She has two yellow bands on her thorax and the top of her abdomen. Her bands can also be white or orange. She has dark-brown wings. The male is a fuzzy greenish yellow all over. His wings are more see-through.

HITCH A RIDE

For lots of bees, tiny insects called *mites* are *bad* news. In honeybee hives, they clamp their mouths onto bees to suck their blood, passing on disease. But *Xylocopa caffra* have a *mutualistic relationship* with one species of mite. The mites ride inside a special "room" in the female bee hosts' bodies and get flown to bee nests, where they can raise their mite babies. In return, the mites eat moldy fungi that might get in the pollen that the bees collect and store for their larvae to eat.

BEE-HAVIOR

These bees act like lots of other carpenter bees. The females are solitary nesters. They dig their nests in plants like aloe, agave, and mallow. The males drone around, looking for females to mate with.

Like other bees that make nests in tube-shaped spaces, *Xylocopa caffra* emerges one bee at a time after they are born. Usually, the bee closest to the entrance is the first one out of the nest. But not with double-banded carpenter bees. The first bee to hatch is the one farthest from the entrance. It clomps its way through the whole nest. On its way, it breaks down the walls of the nest cells where its brothers and sisters are still only larvae. It's like it's yelling, "WAKE UP!" And they do wake up—just for a moment. Then they pretty much go right back to snoozing. They lie piled up all together in their ruined nest until the weather warms up and they are full-grown bees.

There's a long list of plants this species likes to visit, such as amaranth and acacia, eucalyptus and gorse, bougainvillea and senna. That makes farmers interested to know if they can breed these bees to pollinate crops. Bee scientists are experimenting with getting these bees to make their nests in bamboo stems that they can then transfer to farm fields.

There's also a long list of environments these bees like to live in. Some live near the coast. Some live inland in scrubby, dry, hot places.

WHERE?
Africa

SIZE
Almost 1 inch (25 mm) long

Black abdomen

SIDE VIEW

TOP VIEW

▲ *There is no mistaking the two yellow stripes of these double-banded carpenter bee females.*

BEE LOOK-ALIKES:
Don't Be Fooled Again!

Is that *really* a bee? Is it a wasp? Is it . . . something else entirely? Don't be fooled by these impostors. Here are some wanna-bees and how to spot them.

HOVERFLIES

Yellow and black stripes, check. Head, abdomen, and thorax, check. A hoverfly is deceptively bee-like. But flies have big, round compound eyes that take up most of the space on their heads, while bees' compound eyes take up less space. Another clue this is a wanna-bee? The wings: flies have just two forewings, whereas bees have two forewings and two hind wings.

BEE FLIES

This little guy is hairy and chunky like a bumblebee, and it buzzes and hovers like a bee.

But it's really a fly. The clues? You guessed it: just two forewings and the two large compound eyes.

YELLOWJACKETS

Hopefully, you haven't had a run-in with these angry wanna-bees. Their markings make them look like honeybees, but they're definitely not. There are two clues to help you figure out the difference between a yellowjacket—or any wasp—and a bee. One is the yellowjacket's sleek, unhairy body. The other is how its body thins between its abdomen and thorax. Wasps have a thin waist, whereas bees have a stockier body. Stay away from yellowjackets if you can. They nest in the ground and will swarm if they feel threatened.

HOVERFLY

BEE FLY

PAPER WASPS

Paper wasps have stripes just like bees, but you'll recognize their waspy waist and hairless body. They also come in brown, black, orange, or yellow. Another way you can tell a paper wasp from a bee is if it goes home to a paper nest. You can sometimes find these under branches of trees or the eaves of houses.

CICADA KILLER WASPS

Don't be fooled by the stripes! A closer look at this cicada killer wasp's red eyes, brown wings, brown feet, and narrow waist—not to mention its mostly hairless body—will let you know this is not a true bee. It's also not a threat to you! Cicada killer wasps are not as aggressive as other wasps. Well, except to cicadas.

PAPER WASP

YELLOWJACKET

CICADA KILLER WASP

LEAFCUTTER BEES

Family: Megachilidae
Genus: *Megachile*

*M*egachile is the genus that contains the BIGGEST bees there are. One way to remember this is by thinking of their name. It starts with mega, which actually refers to their BIG jaws. These bees have got BIG jaws in addition to their BIG bodies and BIG everything else.

There are 1,400 species of *Megachile* all over the world. They are known as leafcutters because they use their BIG jaws to cut off bits of leaves and flowers and plant matter. They bring these back home and use them to line their nest cells. If you could pull a nest cell out, you would see a snug little leaf or petal roll that a female fills with nectar and pollen to feed her future babies. It also means that you'll only find these bees where their favorite leafy plants and trees exist. No leaves, no *Megachile*.

Most of these (mostly) solitary bees make their nests above the ground. Some of them prefer holes in dead wood. Others prefer to build in the tubelike stems of dead plants. A few of them like to make their nests in the sand. Females rub a special scent at the entrance to their nests. This is how they know they are home.

Most species in this group are generalists. But some are specialists that like a few plants, and a few visit only one kind of special flower. This flower is the evening primrose. It opens its petals at night. So that is when these bees are active too. Other leafcutters, like alfalfa leafcutters, are used by farmers to pollinate crops. Many arrived in the United States accidentally, brought from other countries. They hitched rides in the dead wood they nested in. Then they spread all across the country.

◀ *A leafcutter bee from Malaysia, sprinkled with pollen.*

Bellflower resin bee

Megachile campanulae

ID THIS BEE

The females of this long, skinny species are black and shiny with velvety faces. The males are black too. But they have furry gray heads and thoraxes. Both males and females have narrow white lines on their abdomens. Their wings are tinged brown. Like all *Megachile*, female *Megachile campanulae* have pollen-collecting hairs on their bellies, or scopa. Entomologists say these bees have an "armored" appearance because of how hard and sturdy their exoskeletons look.

ARTIFICIAL INGREDIENTS

Megachile campanulae living in cities might use human-made materials instead of resin to build their nests, such as caulk and plastic. This is called *adaptive behavior*. These bees can't find the natural resources they need, so use whatever they can find. Unfortunately, plastics are toxic and don't "breathe" like natural materials, meaning bees that use them can get sick or suffocate. This is another way humans are changing the environment and making things hard for bees.

BEE-HAVIOR

Like her fellow leafcutter bee species, the female *Megachile campanulae* builds her nest inside hollow stems or holes that were made in trees by other insects. But unlike a lot of other leafcutter bees, *Megachile campanulae* doesn't chomp off bits of leaves to line her nest. In fact, she does not even have the right cutting blades on her jaws to do this. Instead, she lines her nest with resin, just like *Megachile pluto*. She collects this sticky stuff from the plants she visits. Plants such as milkweed, wild indigo, mallow, and the bellflowers she is named for.

Plants ooze out *resin*, which can be colored red, brown, or yellow. In midsummer, when she is most active, a female *Megachile campanulae* collects balls of it in her big jaws. Resin is also waterproof, so it makes good wallpaper for her house. If you were to find a *Megachile campanulae* nest out in the wild, you would be able to tell who made it. A resin-lined nest would be very hard or a little sticky. Unlike a leaf-lined nest, which would be dry and flimsy. If you squeezed a resin nest, it might smell like pine.

Because of the way these bees build their nests, they are considered mason bees in addition to being leafcutter bees and resin bees.

WHERE?

Eastern North America, stretching as far west as Alaska

SIZE

Female: 0.4–0.43 inch (10–11 mm) long

Male: 0.31–0.35 inch

MALE SIDE VIEW

MALE FACE

▲ *The male bellflower resin bee has a furry gray thorax.*

Wallace's giant bee
Megachile pluto

REDISCOVERED

Scientists do not know much about *Megachile pluto*. A British naturalist named Alfred Russel Wallace saw it on a trip to the Bacan Islands in Indonesia in the mid-19th century. It was described a year later by another British scientist named Frederick Smith. Then no one saw it until 1981, when it was found by an American scientist on the Bacan Islands and two other nearby islands called Halmahera and Tidore.

Then, once again, it seemed to go extinct. No one saw *Megachile pluto* in the wild for another 40 years.

But, in 2019, a team of scientists set out to look for it. Their journey was part of a bigger expedition to find 25 species of all kinds that have not been seen for 10 years. They returned to the islands where *Megachile pluto* had been found in the past. They knew the bees lived with termites. So every day, they stared at termite mounds. Inside one of them they found a female *Megachile pluto*. It wasn't extinct after all!

Special care must be taken to make sure that *Megachile pluto* sticks around. One of its biggest threats is *habitat loss*. The forests *Megachile pluto* needs to live in are being cut down for palm-oil plantations. But because the scientists showed that this bee is not extinct, the Indonesian government can now make a conservation program to protect the bees.

ID THIS BEE

This is it. This is officially the biggest bee in the world. At least the females are, anyway. Not only are they very long, but their wingspans are 2.5 inches wide. Females also have huge, powerful jaws that look like the jaws on stag beetles. Males are much smaller. Both male and female bees are mostly black.

BEE-HAVIOR

These amazing-looking insects are a kind of bee known as *resin bees*. The females use those huge jaws to scoop up resin that oozes out of trees. Then they use that resin to build their nest cells. They choose an unusual location to do this: inside the nests of a termite species called *Microcerotermes amboinensis*. Multiple females nest communally inside these termite nests.

Although it forages for nectar and pollen, *Megachile pluto* does not make honey. Too bad. Can you imagine how much honey these big bees could produce?

WHERE?
Indonesia

SIZE
Females: 1.5 inches (38 mm) long
Males: 0.9 inch (23 mm) long

THREATENED!
Vulnerable.

2.5-inch wingspan

FEMALE TOP VIEW

FEMALE SIDE VIEW

▲ *The biggest bee in the world!*

Alfalfa leafcutting bee
Megachile rotundata

A IS FOR ALFALFA

Mature *Megachile rotundata* bees leave their nests in early summer. That is when alfalfa just starts to bloom. This is no coincidence. The success of both these living things is tied together. They need each other to thrive. Alfalfa leafcutters are found all over the United States now. But they arrived back in the 1940s. They often nest in wood, and all kinds of wooden things are imported into the United States. So scientists think the bees hitched a ride.

Sometime after the bees were discovered in the United States, people realized these bees were really good at pollinating alfalfa. Not many bees are small enough to fit inside an alfalfa flower and pick up enough pollen to bring to the next flower to pollinate it. But one small alfalfa leafcutter female can visit enough flowers in the one month of her life to help make a quarter pound of alfalfa seeds. That is a lot more efficient than honeybees. Just like honeybees, alfalfa leafcutters are now raised all over the world to help with pollination services.

Who cares about alfalfa? If you eat beef or drink milk, you do! Alfalfa seeds are planted in pastures where cattle graze. It is a very important food crop for them. Alfalfa is also grown and then cut and dried into hay. This feeds cows and other livestock. It also feeds horses and rabbits and other animals we keep as pets.

ID THIS BEE

Meet the smallest of the leafcutters! Alfalfa leafcutting bees are dark gray. Females have white hairs on their heads. They also have white *scopae* on their bellies. Males have two pale spots on the tips of their abdomens. You will find their nests inside almost anything tubular: beetle holes in dead wood, flower stems, and even drinking straws.

BEE-HAVIOR

Alfalfa leafcutting bees use leaves to line their nests. Their favorites are Virginia creeper, which is a kind of ivy, and leaves from green ash trees. These solitary bees are able to cut two-and-a-half-inch near-perfect circles out of leaves. It is their own special trick.

Like other leafcutters, *Megachile rotundata* lays eggs in tubes. A female might lay as many as 40 eggs in individual nest cells all in a row. Each one gets lined with leaves. The eggs hatch into larvae inside their nests in the middle of winter. They develop into full-grown bees while it is still cold and then emerge into the warmth of summer.

WHERE?
Native to Europe and Asia but now found on all continents except Antarctica

SIZE
0.24–0.35 inch (6–9 mm) long

▶ *An alfalfa leafcutting bee on an alfalfa flower.*

MALE FACE

Sunflower leafcutting bee
Megachile fortis

ID THIS BEE

Look at this amazing huge and shaggy bee! It is actually the largest leafcutter bee in North America. Is it also the shaggiest? Its big, hairy forelegs sure make it look like a good candidate. It is stocky and black and yellow and has five teeth (although you have to get up really close to see those).

▲ Megachile fortis *pollinates everything in the sunflower family.*

BEE-HAVIOR

Megachile fortis is a specialist bee. It likes sunflowers. (You might have guessed that by its common name.) A lot of leafcutter bees nest in wood. Not *Megachile fortis*. It nests in the ground. Like other leafcutters, it uses the teeth in its strong jaws to snip pieces of leaves. It builds nest cells with these bits and bobs.

Here's what else we know about this very cool-looking bee:

It has extra tips on its antennae.

It lives in grasslands.

Those grasslands are disappearing. And so is *Megachile fortis*. It is not listed on any endangered lists. But it is said to be one of the rarest leafcutter bees in Canada. In the United States, it hasn't been seen in four of its native states since 1990.

Megachile fortis is one of many kinds of bees that are vanishing faster than we can study them. We think there are about 4,000 species of native bees in the United States alone. But we know very little about most of them. How many of these bees are left in the wild? Have they found other places to live that we do not know about? Answering these questions is very important. We cannot protect what we do not understand.

WHERE?

Central United States, Canada

SIZE

Female: 0.63–0.7 inch (16–18 mm) long

Male: 0.55–0.6 inch (14–15 mm) long

Shaggy head and thorax

SIDE VIEW

HEAD-ON

▲ Megachile fortis *has distinctive hairy forelegs.*

What's a Nest Cell?

Bees build nests or hives, and those contain cells. You're probably familiar with the hexagonal-shaped wax cells that honeybees build. But solitary bees also build *nest cells*. Depending on the bee, those cells can be made of leaves or bark or resin or mud or even a snail shell.

These cells hold a few things. First, bees store food in their nest cells like pollen and nectar.

Bees also lay eggs in their nest cells. Sometimes those eggs are tended to until they develop into larvae; sometimes the next cells are closed up with the eggs inside and left alone until full-grown bees emerge.

Some bees are very particular about how they build their nests. So much so that researchers can often identify a bee just by the nest it builds. Take a look at these nest cells.

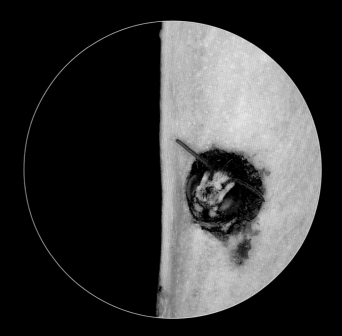

▲ Ashmeadiella *nest.*

▼ Osmia lignaria *developing in mud nest cells.*　　▶ *Different bees make nest cells out of a variety of materials.*

OSMIA

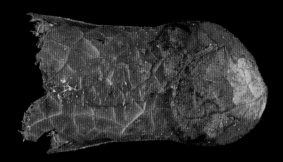

MEGACHILE COCINNA

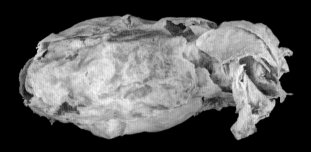

MEGACHILE

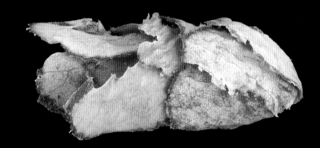

MEGACHILE ROTUNDATA

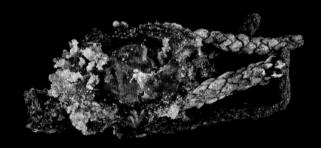

DIANTHIDIUM

DIANTHIDIUM

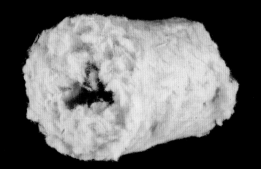

ANTHIDIUM FORMOSUM

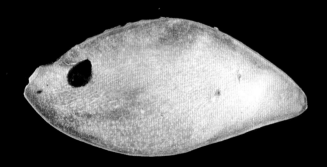

ASHMEADIELLA

SWEAT BEES

Family: Halictidae and four subfamilies: Rophitinae, Nomiinae, Nomioidinae, and Halictinae

Genus: 76 worldwide, including *Halictus, Agapostemon,* and *Lasioglossum*

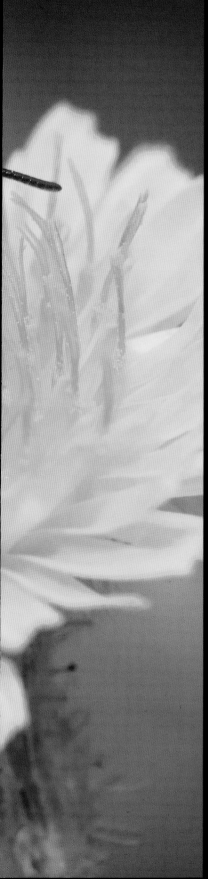

alictidae is a massive family of over 3,500 species. It is split up into four subfamilies that are then split up into 76 genera. One of those subfamilies is Halictinae. Almost all sweat bees belong to this subfamily, including those in the genus *Lasioglossum*. That name means "hairy tongues" in Latin. It is the biggest bee genus of all, made up of 1,800 species around the world and almost 300 in North America.

Some sweat bees use their tongues to lick sweat off humans. One species even licks up human tears and brings them home to feed them to her babies. When they find nice salty sweat or tears, sweat bees make a smell by releasing chemicals called *pheromones*. This signals other bees to come join them. Being surrounded by bees can scare some people. But these bees do not want to hurt you. They just want to lick you! Though, not all sweat bees even like to lick sweat.

There is lots of variety among sweat bees: Some are long. A few are pudgy. Some are long *and* pudgy. Some are parasites. Some are solitary sometimes. They are *eusocial* at other times, with one female bossing other females around so they all work together. Some are solitary when they are up high in the mountains and eusocial at lower elevations. In some species, any female can be a queen. All she has to do is nudge the other females to let them know that she is the boss now.

One subgenus, called *Sphecodogastra*, just likes evening primrose flowers. It has special eyes that can see in the evening and even on full-moon nights, when these flowers open.

But there are some things that sweat bees have in common. They have short tongues. They stash enough pollen and nectar in nest cells for baby bees to eat when they emerge.

◄ *Many sweat bees are jewel toned.*

Ligated furrowed bee
Halictus ligatus

ID THIS BEE

How can you tell a bee in the *Halictus* genus? It has a body that is black or brown. Its abdomen has hairy stripes that appear only on the ends of its segments. *Halictus ligatus* specifically has a jaw that hooks down sharply, like a boomerang shape.

QUEEN WARS

If a foundress dies, a new queen is chosen. Small females are born first in spring. They are usually helpers to their mothers. Big females are born late in the summer. They have lots of fat stores, which make them hardy and strong, and they may go on to become queens. Sometimes a worker wants to be a queen, so she starts laying her own eggs.

If a few queens build nests together, one of them will be the egg layer and the others will be nest guarders and pollen foragers. In rough weather or during a slim flower season, queens may stop cooperating with each other, becoming solitary bees and building separate nests.

BEE-HAVIOR

Halictus ligatus is thought to be the bee that lives in the most places and in the most kinds of climates. That means its behavior is different depending on where it lives. For example, some of these bees nest together, while some build solitary nests.

Halictus ligatus visits *lots* of different kinds of flowers. Some scientists have counted as many as 204 kinds. Asters. Plums. Zinnias. Broccoli. Sunflowers. Being able to forage from a variety of flowers is a good way to survive if one plant disappears.

Halictus ligatus nests in the ground. It likes loose, bare soil because it is easy to dig a hole in. Females will make nests connected to each other. Building in this way makes it hard for parasitic bees to break in. Someone is always watching the entrance. "New" nests are usually tidied-up old nests that were built in years past by mother and grandmother bees. Over the years, the number of tunnels from one nest to another grows and grows.

Queen-like bees of this and similar species are called *foundresses*. A foundress lays a few eggs at a time in one main nest cell. But it is her firstborn daughters that fill the nest cell with a big ball of pollen and nectar. They go out to collect it in the morning and are done for the day by noon. Those daughters will also then build new nest cells. What does their mother do? Aside from lay all the eggs, she guards the entrance to the nest. She can tell if you belong by your smell.

WHERE?
Arctic Circle to Venezuela

SIZE
Female: 0.31–0.4 inch
(8–10 mm) long;
queens are the biggest
Male: 0.27–0.35 inch
(7–9 mm) long

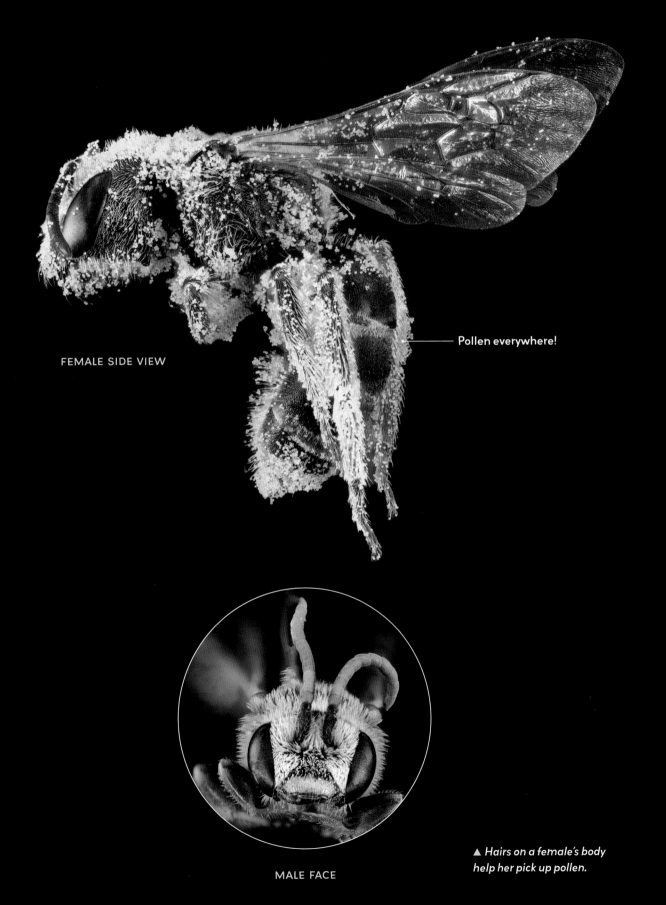

FEMALE SIDE VIEW

Pollen everywhere!

MALE FACE

▲ *Hairs on a female's body help her pick up pollen.*

Angeles striped sweat bee
Agapostemon angelicus

ID THIS BEE

These are medium-size sweat bees. Females are completely metallic green. They have two dents on a part of their thorax called the *scutum*. Males have black-and-yellow-striped abdomens.

BEE-SNOOZY

Even though females build nests in the ground, one scientist observed *Agapostemon angelicus* snoozing at night on sunflowers and dried-out camphorweed flowers. The scientist said he always saw the females sleeping alone. The males slept in groups, with as many as six bees on one flower head. They held on to the flowers with their legs. And they were all covered with dew. Bees can fly when they are wet, but they usually do not like to. Wet wings make them slow and heavy. They have to wait to dry out before they can forage for breakfast.

BEE-HAVIOR

Angeles striped sweat bees are often native to desertlike places. Some of those places are high up, around 12,000 feet above sea level. Some of them are below sea level. That's the biggest range difference based on *altitude* for any bee in North America. One desert flower these bees really like comes from a kind of shrub cactus called Munz's cholla. Angeles striped sweat bees prefer to be out flying and foraging in the morning, when the cholla flowers are open.

But like all bees in the *Agapostemon* genus, these are generalists. They like pollen from many kinds of flowers. (*Agapostemon* means "stamen-loving"; the *stamen* is the part of a flower that makes pollen.) They also like sunflowers and cotton flowers. In fact, they like cotton so much that cotton farmers have wondered if they could raise these bees to pollinate their cotton crops.

They also make their nests in dirt. They burrow in and toss dirt out of the hole. That dirt forms a little pile, called a *tumulus*, all around the hole. The tumulus might help keep rain out of the nest. Sometimes females will make their nests near each other and share an entrance tunnel. But if they can't find any other females to team up with, they'll just make solitary nests.

WHERE?
Western and southwestern United States, northern Mexico

SIZE
0.39–0.51 inch (10–13 mm) long

MALE SIDE VIEW

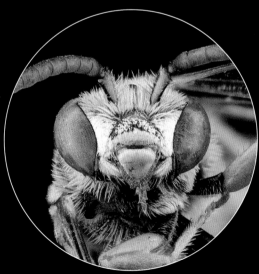

MALE FRONT VIEW

▲ *These sweat bees definitely like to lick your sweat!*

BANDED BEES

Family: Apidae

Genus: *Amegilla*

There are over 250 known species of *Amegilla* bees around the world. There are 27 species in East African countries. There are about 36 species in Europe and North Africa. They mostly live in arid places. That is, places that are quite dry.

Amegilla bees are known as banded bees. If you look at pictures of some species, the reason is clear. These bees have very vivid stripes, or bands, around their abdomens. Those stripes may be colored blue or blue green. Sometimes the bands are not a different color. They are just grooves in the bees' abdomens.

Banded bees are medium-size bees about the size of honeybees. (They do not make honey, though.) They sometimes get described as "rotund," and they also make a loud buzzing noise when they fly.

They don't always use their long tongues to gently slurp flower nectar. Sometimes they rob nectar from tube-shaped flowers. To do this, they stand on the outside of the flower. They poke a hole in the base of it with the sheath around their tongue, and then they soak up the nectar. They do not enter that flower to drink nectar, which means they also do not pollinate that flower. However, they do pollinate some flowers. Like bumblebees, they are buzz pollinators. They hold on to the flower with their legs, then they vibrate or bang their bodies to get pollen to fall on them. One species, *Amegilla murrayensis*, bangs her head 350 times per second to get pollen out of a flower. Bumblebees only make 240 vibrations per second when they buzz-pollinate.

Females dig out nests from mud or sand or sandstone, placing their nests near other blue-banded bee nests. The nest cells are oval shaped. Once the female fills them with pollen and nectar for her future babies, she plugs them with more mud or sand.

◀ *There are 250 species of* Amegilla *around the world.*

Common blue-banded bee
Amegilla cingulata

ID THIS BEE

Here is an amazing-looking banded bee. It has a hairy yellow thorax. It also has pale-metallic-blue stripes on its black abdomen. The females have four stripes, and the males have five. All of them have big green eyes and see-through wings.

WE'RE #1!

Amegilla cingulata may be easy to find in Australia. But it is unique in at least one way. It was the first species of Australian bee to be described by a scientist. That happened all the way back in 1775. The scientist was an entomologist from Denmark named Johan Christian Fabricius. He gave the bee the name *Amegilla cingulata* from the Latin word for "belt."

BEE-HAVIOR

You are likely to spot this bee as it is hovering between flowers. Then the next thing you know, this bee will be darting straight to a pollen source. It is very common all over mainland Australia, where it lives in cities. It also lives in tropical forests and heathlands. A *heathland* is similar to a grassland, only it grows just a few shrubby plants, such as heather and lavender. *Amegilla cingulata* is one of a number of species of *Amegilla* in Australia. You can find them everywhere but Tasmania, an island off the southern coast of the country.

Amegilla cingulata favors sandstone as nest material, although she might also make her nest in mud bricks. Besides *Amegilla cingulata* babies, there is someone else who really likes her nests. That is the neon cuckoo bee, *Thyreus nitidulus* (see page 44).

Scientists once thought that the common blue-banded bee only visited blue and purple flowers. Now we know this is not true. After all, they pollinate tomato flowers, for example. Tomato flowers are white or yellow. However, blue-banded bees still seem to like flowers of the lavender plant more than others. Some people report that these bees are also drawn to them when they wear blue clothes. But these bees are quite gentle. And they fly solo instead of in groups or swarms. So there is no need to fear when they come near.

WHERE?

Native to Australia, except Tasmania; also found in Papua New Guinea, Malaysia, and India

SIZE

0.39–0.47 inch
(10–12 mm) long

Translucent wings

FEMALE SIDE VIEW

Metallic-blue stripes
on black abdomen

▲ *There's nothing "common" looking about
the beautiful common blue-banded bee.*

ID THIS BEE

This medium-size chonker is named for the very shaggy and thick reddish-gold fur all over its head and body. Younger bees are the furriest. As they get older, some of the fur wears away. Then you can see the smooth, dark bands (stripes) on their abdomens. Females have six bands. Males have seven bands. Some of the fur on their back legs is also dark colored. Their green eyes are the color of jade. Some subspecies have eyes the color of emeralds.

GOOD-NIGHT BEES

Male teddy bear bees do not sleep in a nest. Instead, they chomp onto twigs on trees or blades of grass. When one male flies in to join another, they both wave their legs and wiggle their bodies. Four or five males may hang close together on a single twig. When it is time to sleep, they tuck their legs up under their bodies. They will rest like this all night long. Sleep tight and sweet dreams, boys.

BEE-HAVIOR

Teddy bear bees are sometimes known as *golden digger* bees. This is because, number one, as you can see, they have golden fur. And number two, like all *Amegilla* bees, the females dig nests in the ground. Teddy bear bees tend to prefer making their nests with mud, although some scientists have noticed that they often make nests in the dirt underneath human houses.

Teddy bear bees are thought to have many of the same behaviors as common blue-banded bees. This makes sense because they are closely related. But we know very little about the way they mate. We also don't know what their favorite flowers are or what behaviors they show in the wild.

Teddy bear bees actually belong to a subgenus of banded bees called *Asaropoda*. In that subgenus, there are several species of teddy bear bees—and scientists have been finding new ones. In fact, they have found five new teddy bear bee species since 2010. The latest species was found on a hibiscus flower in 2017. It is possible that there are even more teddy bear bee species out there waiting for discovery.

▶ *Teddy bear bees are very hairy.*

WHERE?

Native to eastern Australia, Indonesia, and Papua New Guinea

SIZE

0.6–0.79 inch (15–20 mm) long

Eyes the color of jade or emeralds

Shaggy, reddish-gold fur

Other Pollinators

Some bees are pretty perfect pollinators because their bodies are covered in hairs that pick up pollen and help transport it around the inside of a flower and also from plant to plant. Although bees are some of the busiest, buzziest, and best pollinators, there are plenty of others doing their part for plants. Check out these pollinator profiles:

Butterflies: These beauties drink up flower nectar with a long proboscis, and as they do, they collect pollen on their legs and bodies. Unlike bees, butterflies can see the color red, so they're drawn to red and orange flowers, which are usually passed up by bees.

Beetles: Beetles munch their way through flower parts—and even poop on them—to get to the nectar inside. And all the while, they get coated in pollen. Because of this, beetles are sometimes known as "mess and soil" pollinators. Beetles help pollinate white and green flowers, such as magnolias or waterlilies; plants with a fruity scent; and those with big bowl shapes and an exposed stamen and pistil.

Moths: When the sun goes down and most other pollinators go to sleep, moths take over! There are

BEETLES BEFORE BEES

Beetles were some of the first pollinators on Earth! Fossils dating 200 million years ago show that beetles visited ancient plants in the Mesozoic era.

MONARCH BUTTERFLY

ANTS IN A EUCALYPTUS FLOWER

many nocturnal (active at night) species of moths, and they feed on flowers that open in the late afternoon and evenings. They tend to like plants with white or dull flowers, such as morning glory, yucca, and gardenia.

Flies: Yes, flies help pollinate plants too. They tend to like dull-brown or purple flowers or ones with tricky shapes, like orchids. They also like flowers that stink; plants that smell like rot, fungus, blood, or poop don't bother these pollinators. You might find them on jack-in-the-pulpit, pawpaw, or skunk cabbage. Hey, somebody's got to pollinate these stinkers!

Wasps: These bee look-alikes are also important pollinators, although they don't do the job as well as bees do. Wasps need a lot of nectar and pollen to fuel their flying, so they visit a wide variety of plants.

NON-INSECT POLLINATORS

Here are some other animals that do their part to keep plants producing:

Birds
Bats
Slugs
Gnats
Lemurs

Geckos
Skinks
Lizards
Honey possums

Ants: Some (but not all) ants are important pollinators of low-growing plants with small flowers and witchy-sounding names like Cascade knotweed and alpine nailwort.

NEW HOLLAND HONEYEATER

BROWN ANOLE LIZARD

Dawson's burrowing bee
Amegilla dawsoni

ID THIS BEE

These are some of the biggest bees in Australia. Males come in two different sizes: small and large. Both males and females have fur. But males have light-brown fur. Females have white fur on their heads and thoraxes. They have yellow face markings and reddish-brown abdomens.

FIGHT TO THE DEATH

New female bees dig their way out of their nests, ready to visit flowers and build nests for their own future babies. But what they find are males waiting to fight each other to be the bee that gets to mate with the females. They fight to the death by biting and stinging. Sometimes they fight on top of the female's head, or they cluster around her in a big ball. At the end of battle, many of the big males are dead. Meanwhile, the small males have another strategy: they wait by the flowers for new females to arrive.

BEE-HAVIOR

Female Dawson's bees make their nests in the hard red mudflats in the western Australian outback. As many as 10,000 females might dig their nests next to each other in one big colony. From the air, the nests look like thousands of tiny chimneys sticking up from the ground. That shape serves a purpose. It keeps dirt from falling into the nest.

To make their burrows, females first have to soften up the hard ground. They use nectar to do this. Then they bite the dirt to make perfectly round holes. As they keep biting, the holes turn into long tunnels that end in nest cells. Those nest cells get lined with wax to make them waterproof. Each cell is then filled with pools of pollen and nectar. The female lays her egg on top. It floats there until it hatches. Then the baby bee larva drinks the nectar it is lying in until the nectar is all gone. That takes a week. Then the larva sleeps through the winter. When the adult bee emerges, it is July, and the poverty bush and rough bluebell flowers are blooming in the barren landscape.

▲ *Dawson's, burrowing!*

▶ **Amegila dawsoni** *nests dug next to each other to make up one big colony.*

WHERE?
Western Australia

SIZE
Up to 0.9 inch (23 mm) long

White-banded digger bee
Amegilla quadrifasciata

▲ *Female* Amegilla quadrifasciata.

▶ *Foraging white-banded digger bee.*

BEE-HAVIOR

In some cases, scientists know so little about some bee species they cannot even say if there are many of that bee in its native range, or if its population is declining, or if it has already disappeared. Knowing this is important. Some native and solitary bees pollinate only certain plants. Without the bees' pollination services, those plants may go extinct. Now flip that around. If the plants are ripped up to make way for houses and roads, certain bees may go extinct. Both these actions change ecosystems—communities of interacting organisms—and we never fully understand what the effects of those changes will be.

Scientists know enough about *Amegilla quadrifasciata to* say that there is plenty of this species flying around some parts of Europe especially. They have seen it flying over shrublands in Greece. They have found it in salt marshes in France. It has been spotted on farms in Italy. Scientists assume it likes many different kinds of plants, such as verbena and borage. And they are pretty sure it is a solitary nester. But to know any more, they would have to study this bee up close for a while. That hasn't happened yet—which means that we do not know how it is affected by human actions.

WHERE?
Japan, central Asia, North Africa, southern Europe

SIZE
0.35–0.47 inch (9–12 mm) long

THREATENED!
Presumed extinct in some parts of Germany

LONG-HORNED BEES

Eucerini tribe
Family: Apidae
Genus: *Eucera,*
Melissodes,
and 30 others

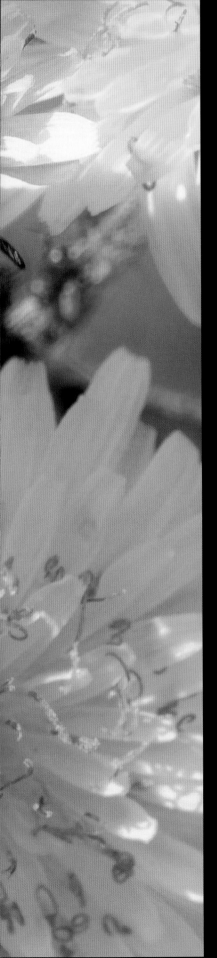

Eucerini is a tribe of bees. A tribe sits between a family and a genus, and it contains two or more genera. Those genera share a *common ancestor*. And from that ancestor, the genera may inherit a trait that links them together. In this case, that trait is the "long horns" that give these bees their name. Actually, it is only the males that have very long antennae—not horns at all.

Even though they have a common ancestor, species in the Eucerini tribe are more different from each other than any other in the whole Apidae family. There are 14 genera and 200 species of them in North America alone. There are 300 species of *Eucera* in Europe, Asia, and India and 62 species in North America. There are 125 species of *Melissodes*. They live only in North and South America. But two very cool genera are *Peponapis* and *Xenoglossa*, which are specialist bees. They only visit squash flowers. For this reason, they are known as *squash bees*.

Many Eucerini species are specialist bees. One species only visits pickerelweed flowers. Another only cactus flowers. Another only morning glories. Some species of *Eucera* only visit flowers in the pea family or only wild orchids. Some species of *Melissodes* only sunflowers or thistles. The bees in these genera are medium to large in size and are hairy. Almost all are solitary ground nesters. But *Eucera* emerges in very early spring, whereas *Melissodes* emerges in late summer or early autumn.

Some *Melissodes* males will sleep clinging to stems, like banded bee males do. Others may cram into cracks in rocks. Male squash bees crawl into squash flowers to forage. The flowers close in the heat of the day, and the males get trapped inside. They do not panic. Instead, they nap there until morning. Sometimes young female squash bees like to sleep inside flowers too.

◄ *A member of the Eucerini tribe,* Eucera longicornis.

Long-horned bee
Eucera longicornis

THE BETTER TO SMELL YOU WITH

Eucera males have very long antennae. But why on Earth would they need such things? Scientists think it is to help them smell better. In particular, they need to smell females in order to mate with them. This means they can also be tricked. A special kind of orchid makes a smell that is like that of female bees. When the males smell it, they fly to the flower. No female bee there! This is how the orchid tricks the bee into pollinating it.

BEE-HAVIOR

Here is a bee that *loves* flowers in the pea family, which includes vetch flowers, clover flowers, and a flower with a funny name: bird's-foot trefoil. The bees need to visit pea flowers for three to six weeks so that they can get enough pollen to provision their nests. If they emerge before these flowers are blooming, they may go back to bed to wait until the flowers are ready. That's because the pollen in these flowers is special. It is very high in the protein the bees need to thrive.

But many pea plant species are disappearing. That means the bees are disappearing too. They used to be found in 30 places in Britain's Cornwall region. Now they are found in just 12. They can travel only 2,000 feet away from their nests to forage. That means bees cannot just visit another neighborhood to get the food they need.

When no pea flowers are around, the bees may visit bramble flowers, heather, or geraniums. However, pollen from these plants does not have enough protein for the babies to develop just right, and it may be hard for them to digest.

Eucera longicornis lives in grasslands and heathlands and near forests. It really prefers to build its nests in the sides of clay cliffs, though. Females dig holes that face south. That way, they feel the warm sun first thing in the morning. They are solitary. But they are also communal and may build their nests near other nests.

WHERE?
Southern Britain, Europe all the way to China

SIZE
0.39–0.51 inch (10–13 mm) long

THREATENED!
UK Priority Species

▲ Eucera longicornis *front view.*

▶ *Resting on a flower.*

Squash bee
Xenoglossa strenua

THE BEST NEST

Different species of bees have different ways they build their nests. These squash bee females first burrow straight down. They dig out about three nest cells that they coat with a special wax to make them waterproof. Then they start burrowing again at a 90-degree angle. They put in a few more nest cells. Then they start burrowing down again—only at a 45-degree angle this time. Then another zigzag across and down. A cross section of a nest looks like a weird collection of pipes underneath a sink that all end in fat fingers.

BEE-HAVIOR

Here is a kind of squash bee that lives in warm places in the United States. That includes California, Virginia, Texas, and Florida. It also prefers low *elevations*. That means not high up in the mountains but lower down, near sea level.

Squash bees are fast fliers. And this species is an early riser. It is up and at 'em as the sun is rising, when the temperatures are still on the cool side. Most females are finished collecting nectar and pollen by 7:00 a.m. Good luck finding these bees out and about much later than 8:00 a.m.

For easy access to the food they need to live, many of these bees build their nests right next to squash fields. The nests are burrows in the ground that have tall chimneys on top of them. Whenever a bee returns to her nest to rest, she fills the entrance hole with dirt. At nighttime when she is ready to sleep, she adds more dirt into the entrance hole. That is one way to keep out intruders. But that means she has to dig her way out into the sun every morning. She also uses dirt to plug up nest cells. She does this after she has laid her eggs on a mixture of nectar and pollen, with some pollen crumbs sprinkled on top.

WHERE?

North America

SIZE

Female: 0.55–0.7 inch (14–18 mm) long

Male: 0.55–0.61 inch (14–15.5 mm) long

FEMALE TOP VIEW

FEMALE FACE

▲ *Squash bees visit flowers of their preferred plants—squashes.*

Bees under Threat . . . and How to Help

As you've seen throughout this book, many bee populations are declining in number, and some species are endangered. Bees and pollinators face many threats, but there are things you can do to help them too! Here are some of the dangers bees face and easy things you can do every day to help them:

Habitat loss: As humans build over natural land and as climate change alters the makeup of landscapes worldwide, bees are losing their habitat due to habitat loss, degradation, and fragmentation. Habitat loss happens when an area of land gets radically changed—think about an apartment building being built in a formerly grassy area. Habitat degradation happens when the quality of a habitat gets worse—such as when a garden of native plants and flowers is replaced by one without bee-friendly flowers. Habitat fragmentation happens when a habitat gets split up—for example, a highway and some roads are built through the middle of a field. The new parcels of land might not be enough to feed and house the pollinators.

How to help: Plant those pollinator-friendly gardens, and ask your neighbors to as well! Also, support wild spaces and oppose building on precious land for native pollinators.

Pesticides: Although pesticides keep crop-killing insects away, they also poison pollinators. Some researchers have found over 150 different chemicals in bee pollen! This mixture can be deadly for bees.

How to help: Buy organic produce at the store—produce that doesn't get treated with synthetic pesticides. Reach out to your legislators and ask them to support rules to ban pesticides that harm pollinators.

Pollution: Researchers in India found that air pollution can kill Asian honeybees. By studying more than 1,500 bees in polluted areas, they found that pollution sticks to the bees' bodies and that bees in polluted areas have irregular heartbeats and poor immune systems. Worse yet, four out of five bees that researchers collected in very polluted areas died soon after collection.

How to help: Be as green as you can be! Reduce your own air pollution by walking or riding your bike to school, taking the bus, or riding carpool instead of driving solo.

Global warming: Temperatures are rising around the world, and researchers have found that more frequent hot days—and hotter hot days—affect bumblebees. Superhot days cause bumblebee populations to decline and keep them from colonizing new areas. In fact, bumblebee populations dropped by 46 percent in North America in recent years compared with the years between 1901 and 1974. Warming is also making some flowers bloom early, before the bees are out. When the bees are born, they can find they are too late to get much nectar and pollen.

How to help: Conserve energy as much as you can, and ask those around you to as well.

▶ *Habitat loss is threatening bees and other vital species.*

DIGGER BEES

Anthophorini tribe
Family: Apidae
Genus: *Anthophora* and *Habropoda*

Here, again, is a tribe that has different genera and lots of species. There are seven genera of *Anthophorini* around the world. There are 700 species altogether. The genus *Anthophora* has 400 species. Another genus is *Habropoda,* which has more than 50 species. When we talk about "digger bees," the species in these genera are the ones we mean. If you guessed that they got their name because they dig, you are right! They make their nests in dirt in the ground or sometimes in sand. They dig at it with their front legs. *Anthophora* might make nests of several cells. *Habropoda* makes nests of one cell only.

The females aren't the only ones that dig. Male *Habropoda* bees dig when they hear a new female getting ready to emerge from her nest. They dig down to her so that they can be the first one to mate with her. Sometimes *Habropoda* larvae do not emerge in spring. And then they do not emerge the next spring. They may not emerge until 7 or 10 years have gone by. Scientists think this happens mostly in places where it does not rain very much. If there is not a lot of rain, then there might not be a lot of flowers. If the bees stay in the ground in dry years, they can wait to be born until wet years, when plenty of flowers are blooming to feed them. This could be a way to keep the species from going extinct in dry years.

These bees like cool weather, when other bees do not want to fly. Could it be all that hair on their bodies that keeps them toasty? Maybe. But scientists say they are also able to shiver their bodies in order to warm themselves up. Their hair does have another specific purpose. It picks up lots of pollen. That makes digger bees really good pollinators. They are buzz pollinators, like bumblebees and banded bees.

◄ *A female digger bee in flight.*

Hairy-footed flower bee
Anthophora plumipes

ID THIS BEE

Males are covered all over with shocking gray fuzz, or sometimes its reddish colored. Either way, it looks like they have a bad case of static electricity! They also have very long, "feathery" hairs on their middle legs. They have light markings on their faces. In the United Kingdom, females are black all over with orange-red hairs on their back legs. In the United States, they have very shaggy grayish heads, shaggy golden stripes on their abdomens, and shaggy back legs.

BREAK-INS

Hairy-footed flower bees sometimes make their nests in dirt. But they prefer to make their nests in mortar between bricks. Even though they are solitary, they can make huge communities of nests that can be very noisy. People in England sometimes find these bees inside their houses. Bee researchers say they nested in the mortar in the chimney. Then they accidentally fell down the stack.

BEE-HAVIOR

There is one easy way that people are able to tell the difference between a hairy-footed flower bee and a bumblebee. It's the way they fly. Bumblebees drowse along like they are heavy and sleepy. Flower bees zip and zoom like they are in a hurry to get where they are going. In the United Kingdom, they are probably headed for purple-y lungwort flowers. But they also like comfrey and primrose. They often fly for the flowers with their tongues sticking out.

These bees emerge early in the year. The males come out in late February. They do not mind when the weather is a bit chilly. The females come out one or two weeks later. Females have pollen baskets on their back legs. That makes it easy to carry pollen home to their nests to get ready for baby bees.

These bees are now found in the mid-Atlantic United States. But they are not native to this region. In the 1980s, they were brought to a bee research lab in Maryland. The plan was to study them to see if they could be used to pollinate crops. Now they are found in the wild all over Maryland and Washington, DC.

WHERE?
Europe, England, Asia, North Africa; introduced into the United States and found in Washington, DC, and Maryland

SIZE
0.55–0.6 inch (14–15 mm) long

Gray fuzz all over body

MALE SIDE VIEW

▲ *A male hairy-footed flower bee.*

MINING BEES

Family: Andrenidae
Genus: *Andrena* and 40 others

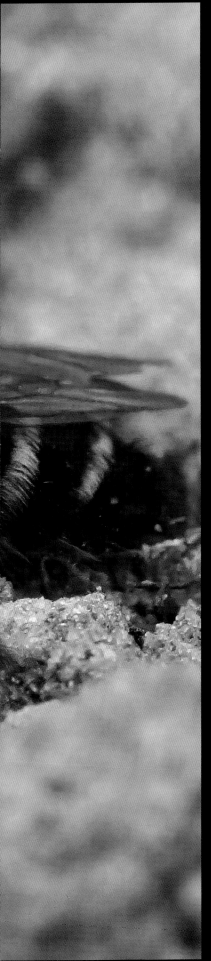

This is the largest bee family in the world. There are about 4,500 species of mining bees. They live everywhere but Australia. They all "mine" their nests straight down into the ground. Nest cells branch off a main tunnel and are lined with waterproofing to protect eggs from moisture and bacteria. How deep the tunnels go depends on the bee. Some only dig a few inches. One bee digs nine feet!

Some of the bees in this family fly at night instead of during the day. One of its 40 genera includes some of the smallest bees we know. The "world's smallest bee" might be US desert native *Perdita minima*. It is so small that entomologists search for it by looking for its longer shadow moving across the landscape. The family has some really big bees too. The genus *Oxaeinae* has some species that are 1 inch (26 mm) long. They are thick and sturdy and fly fast. In the field, you might hear them before you see them.

Several genera of mining bees live in the United States. One of them is *Perdita*. They nest in sand dunes in places like Florida. Instead of lining their nests to make them waterproof, they cover the pollen for their babies with a goo that makes it moldproof. They do not travel more than 200 feet from their nests to forage in flowers. They cannot. They are too small to go far.

Some species may share a nest entrance for their individual nests. Sometimes there are as many as 2,000 nests in one small area. But they all look exactly alike. A female bee has to fly over her nest hole every time she leaves it. She is trying to remember which one belongs to her so that she can recognize it when she gets home.

◄ *A yellow-legged mining bee outside her nest.*

Death camas miner bee
Andrena astragali

▲ Andrena astragali *pollinates.*
a toxic plant called death camas.

BEE-HAVIOR

The Latin name of this bee suggests that it specializes in a species of *Astragalus*. And it is often found buzzing around a species of *Astragalus* called *locoweed*. That plant got its name for the crazy (or "loco") way animals act when they eat it. It is a toxic plant that can cause brain damage and other illnesses.

But the common name of this bee tells another story. Scientists have found out that it is an *oligolege*, meaning it specializes in one flower or one genus of flowers. It does not specialize in locoweed but, instead, another kind of toxic plant called *death camas*. How did entomologists figure this out? They examined 70 female bees that were collected from four states between the years 1933 and 1990. They studied their pollen loads. That is, the pollen they were carrying when they were collected by scientists. Every single pollen load carried pollen from death camas flowers. Some of those loads were 80 percent death camas pollen.

How can these bees eat the nectar and pollen of toxic species and not get sick or die? Some scientists think they forage pollen from the flowers but do not eat it themselves. They leave balls of it in nest cells for their future babies. But then, how are the bee larvae able to eat the toxic pollen? Some scientists believe death camas bees have special powers and can eat the flowers' nectar and pollen and live to fly another day.

WHERE?

North America

SIZE

Female: 0.4–0.51 inch (10–13 mm) long

Male: 0.31–0.47 inch (8–12 mm) long

FEMALE SIDE VIEW

FEMALE TOP VIEW

▲ *The death camas miner bee is a specialist bee.*

Ashy mining bee
Andrena cineraria

HISTORICAL BEES

The genus *Andrena* lives over the world. But for a long time, scientists weren't sure how old the genus was. Then they discovered a fossil. The fossil had been collected from a lake in southern France and was sitting in a museum collection. Some scientists decided to study it. The fossil dated all the way back to the Oligocene epoch. That was a period that started almost 34 million years ago. It was a time when life on Earth began to change dramatically. Our planet was getting cooler. Horses and the first elephants with trunks appeared. Old species were dying out, and many, many new species were appearing— including many grasses and insects. One of those insects was a bee. It got stuck in lake mud and was preserved for millions of years. It told the scientists some important things. The size and pointy shape of its wings told them the bee belonged to the genus *Andrena*. The species, which the scientists called *antoinei*, had been extinct for a long time. But now they knew that its genus was very old indeed.

ID THIS BEE

Females are blue black with two gray hairy stripes on their thoraxes. Males are blue black, too, but that gray hair covers their thoraxes. They also have a tuft of white hair on their faces. It looks like a big bushy mustache.

BEE-HAVIOR

These bees are another cold-loving species. They emerge in early spring, just in time for fruit trees, such as apple and cherry trees. But they like lots of other early-spring flowers, too, such as buttercups, hawthorn, and rapeseed.

Rapeseed is planted in many places as a crop. Farmers sell it to be made into cooking oil. You might see it in the store with the label "canola oil." Ashy mining bees will forage from these plants. But research shows that this may not be good for them. Bees that pollinate rapeseed fields have larvae that grow to be smaller in size. They also produce fewer bees. The pollen in rapeseed may be too low in protein for these bees to thrive.

WHERE?

Europe, United Kingdom

SIZE

0.6 inch (15 mm) long, with males slightly shorter and slimmer than females

MALE FACE

▲ Andrena cineraria *resting on a leaf.*

◄ Male ashy mining bee with big bushy mustache.

OTHER BEES
Hawaiian yellow-faced bees
Genus: *Hylaeus*

ID THIS BEE

These are very small, smooth-ish black bees that look like tiny wasps. They zip around—fast. Males have little yellow dots in between their eyes. Some females have yellow stripes on their faces.

SCOPA VERSUS CORBICULA

A *scopa* is usually a bristly brush of hairs that certain bees have to pick up pollen grains. They can be found in different places on different bee bodies. Other bees have pollen baskets. The scientific name for this little sac is *corbicula,* and it's located on the back of bees' legs. Parasitic bees do not have *scopae* or *corbiculae.* That is because they don't collect any pollen. As we learned earlier, they "steal" it from other bees.

BEE-HAVIOR

All 63 species of these solitary bees that live in Hawaii came from one ancient ancestor. They live on every island and in every kind of landscape on those islands. That means on mountaintops, in forests, and near the ocean. Five species of the 63 in this group are *kleptoparasites*. They sneak their eggs into other bees' nests.

Hawaii's yellow-faced bees don't have much hair on their heads or bodies. Since they carry pollen in their crops instead. A *crop* is the part of a bee stomach that is sometimes called their "honey sack," which many bees use for carrying nectar. These bees are important pollinators of plants that grow only on the islands, such as native geraniums and silversword.

One species, *Hylaeus anthracinus,* lives in the holes of coral that washes up on the beach. Some other species prefer to make nests in holes in wood.

For the first time ever, in 2016, the United States listed bees on its Endangered Species list. Those bees were seven Hawaiian *Hylaeus* species. They were losing habitat. And invasive species of flowers were replacing the native flowers the bees need for foraging. There were other invaders from far away, including ants that ate bee larvae and the bees' favorite flowers. But also rats. And goats, pigs, and sheep that humans brought.

WHERE?

Hawaiian Islands

SIZE

0.23 inch (6 mm) long

CONSERVATION STATUS

Seven species are federally endangered in the United States:

Hylaeus anthracinus
Hylaeus assimulans
Hylaeus facilis
Hylaeus hilaris
Hylaeus kuakea
Hylaeus longiceps
Hylaeus mana

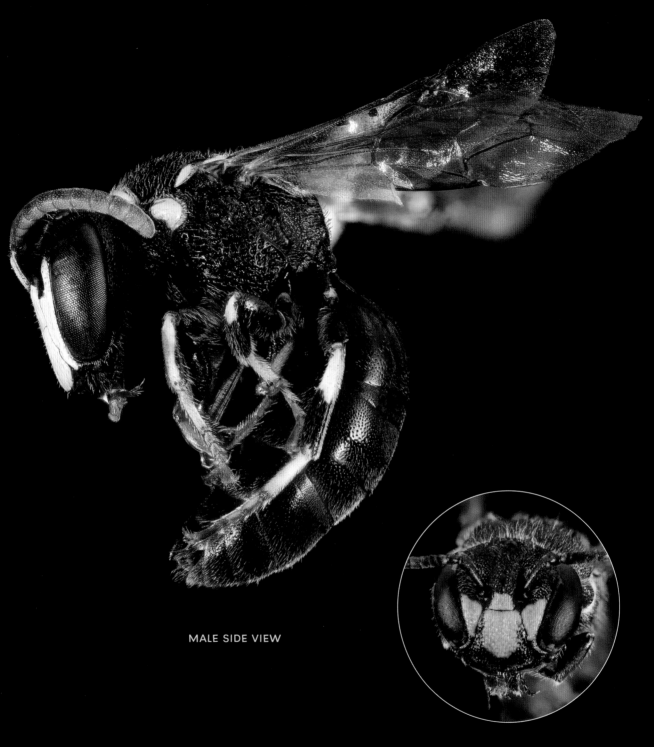

MALE SIDE VIEW

FEMALE FACE

▲ *Hawaiian yellow-faced bees do*
not have scopae or corbiculae.

So Many More Bees!

In this book, you've gotten up close with more than 50 types of bees from around the world. That leaves just 19,950 more bee species to learn about! From solitary bees that go it alone to colonies thousands of bees strong, to crazy-colored cuckoo bees to itty-bitty dwarf bees, the wide world of bees is full of surprises. Keep exploring and IDing those bees, and do your part to help pollinators! Here are some resources to help:

The Xerces Society for Invertebrate Conservation
https://www.xerces.org
This international nonprofit provides tons of information on invertebrates and how to help them. It has special initiatives aimed at helping pollinators, such as the Pollinator Protection Pledge, and it provides opportunities for joining community science programs.

Bee Informed Partnership
https://beeinformed.org
This group is all about helping honeybees. It works with beekeepers and researchers to learn what's best for bees in the long run.

Honey Bee Health Coalition
https://honeybeehealthcoalition.org
This is a collaboration among more than 40 different groups, all dedicated to finding solutions for helping honeybees, native bees, and pollinators and making sure farming systems and natural ecosystems are healthy. Learn what this group is doing to help bees, and learn how you can help bees too!

Bumble Bee Watch
https://www.bumblebeewatch.org
Help scientists track and conserve bumblebees in North America! You can upload photos, ID your bees, and help scientists learn more about endangered bee populations.

◀ *Buy yourself an eco house to attract wild bees.*

▶ *Plant bee-friendly flowers.*

Glossary

adaptive behavior: A way of acting that an animal learns, that helps it to survive

altitude: How high something is, compared to the ground at sea level

apiary/apiarist: A place where bees are kept/a person who keeps bees

brood: Baby bees grow through three stages: eggs, larvae, pupae. All together these stages are known as brood.

catastrophic: In which something terrible and destructive happens, all of a sudden

climate change: The warming that is happening to our planet. It is causing unpredictable weather that threatens the future of all species.

colony/colonial: Some bees live together in groups that work together to survive—a colony. Bees that live this way in a colony are called *colonial*.

commercial: Something that is done for money. A commercial beekeeper raises bees for money.

common ancestor: You and your cousin have the same grandmother—she is your common ancestor, the person who makes you related to each other. Two or more bee species might have a common ancestor that goes back hundreds or thousands of years.

compound eye: An eye made up of lots of tiny eyes. Each of them can look in a different direction

conservation: The protection of nature. That can mean a species of bee, the flowers those bees take nectar from, the prairie where those bees and flowers live, or the clean waters they all need to survive.

corbicula: A "basket" on some bees' hind legs for carrying pollen. It's also known as a pollen basket.

crop: A place in bees' throats for storing nectar until they can get it back to their nests

deforestation: When a lot of trees in a forest are chopped down and that habitat disappears forever *See conservation*

domesticated: When wild animals are kept and raised by humans, they become tame or, at least, used to humans. This may cause them to change their behavior. For example, they may not be able to live in the wild anymore. Honeybees kept by beekeepers are domesticated.

drone: A male bee

endangered: When a species becomes so rare that it might die out and go extinct

endophallus: The part of a male bee he uses to mate with a queen

entomologist: A scientist who studies insects

eusocial: In bees, behavior in which a queen and some males and young females live together and share the work of the nest

extinct: When an entire species has died out. *Tyrannosaurus rex* is extinct. So is the green carpenter bee in southern Australia.

forage/trapline foraging: To forage is to go out and find food in the wild. Some bees visit the same flowers, in the same order, over and over while those flowers last. That is called *trapline foraging*. Scientists think the order might be the shortest distance between flowers.

foundress: A queen bee that has survived through a winter

gallery: Name for a carpenter bee nest

generalist: In bees, a species that likes many different kinds of flowers—as opposed to a specialist

gyne: A female bee that is able to have babies and who will develop into a queen

habitat/habitat loss: A place where an animal lives, like a forest or a meadow or a desert, is a habitat. It contains everything that animal needs to survive, like shelter and food. When a forest is cut down or destroyed by fire or storms, that is called habitat loss. *See deforestation and conservation*

heathland: A wide-open habitat that is covered mostly with low shrubs

hibernation: When an animal lies dormant through the winter without eating or moving. This helps it conserve energy until there is food to eat.

introduced: When a living thing is not native to a place but brought from somewhere else

invasive: When an introduced species starts to breed in its new place and use the resources that native species need to live. Invasive species can wipe out many native plants and animals and also change their habitats.

invertase: A chemical produced in honeybee salivary glands. It helps turn nectar into honey.

kleptoparasite: An animal that steals resources from another animal. In bees, these species often sneak their eggs into other species' nests.

mites: Many species of tiny insect that are related to ticks. Often, mites are bad news for bees because they can cause diseases. But not always! *See mutualistic relationship*

mutualistic relationship: When two species benefit from each other—like double-banded carpenter bees and a species of mite. Or squash bees and squash flowers.

native: A species that comes from the place where you find it. Polar bears are native to Alaska. Honeybees are native to Europe.

nectar: A sweet liquid made by flowers and some plants

nest cell: With bees, a tiny room that a queen lays an egg in

oligolege: A bee that likes one kind of flower or group of flowers. *See specialist*

ovipositor: In female bees, a tube that's used to lay eggs

pheromones: Scented chemical some bees release to signal to other bees

pollen: Powdery stuff found inside flowers, which flowers use to reproduce. That is, make more flowers.

pollination/buzz pollination: When pollen is transferred from the male part of one flower to the female part of another flower of the same species. This fertilizes the flower so it can make seeds. Those seeds drop into the ground so they can grow into more plants bearing more flowers. Some bees, like bumblebees, use buzz pollination when they visit flowers, shaking or banging to knock pollen onto their bodies.

queen: A female bee that can reproduce. That is, lay eggs to make babies.

resin: A thick sticky substance produced by trees. Also known as pitch.

scopa: Hairs on the bellies of bees that catch pollen and help bees move it from place to place. Also known as a pollen brush.

scutum: Part of a bee thorax. It's also how scientists can tell a bee's age. The older the bee is the more hair has worn off its scutum.

social: With bees, those that live in communities.

solitary: With bees, those that live alone.

specialist: A bee that visits one or just a few species of flower. The bees and the flowers often have a special relationship; they need each other to survive. *See mutualistic relationship*

superorganism: A group that acts like one individual. For example, a honeybee colony is made up of thousands of honeybees. They need to work together for the colony to survive. Their colony is a superorganism.

threatened: When a species has become rare enough that it might become endangered and close to extinction

tumulus: A little mound of dirt that piles up as certain bees dig their nests in the ground. It might help keep heavy rains from pouring into the nest.

worker: In a colony of bees, a female that cannot have babies. Instead, she does jobs around the hive: feeding babies, cleaning, taking care of the queen, building honeycomb, and collecting nectar and pollen.

Index

Credits

Lela Nargi is the author of science books for kids, including *The Honeybee Man* (Schwartz & Wade, 2011, illustrated by Kyrsten Brooker), *Absolute Expert: Volcanoes* and *Absolute Expert: Dinosaurs* (National Geographic, 2018), and two upcoming books of opposites. She's also a journalist, and her work has appeared in the *Washington Post* KidsPost, *Science News for Students*, *Highlights*, *Muse*, and many other publications for children (and adults). She lives in Brooklyn, New York, with her family and two bunnies.